"Practical, authentic, and undeniably helpful, *Secrets of Greek Mysticism* needs to be on every spiritual practitioner's bookshelf. Inside you'll find straightforward ways to live in devotion to the earth while also expanding your spiritual perspective. Lizos helps us access the deeper essence of the gods. Our connection with them becomes robust, unbreakable. Many popular texts reduce the gods and goddesses of the Greek pantheon to caricatures—not so this book. Here we find richness, complexity, love. One thing I especially adore about the works of George Lizos is his ability to get straight to the point. Many spiritual guides take 150 pages to say what they should have said in five. Not so with this book. Everything in this book brings substance. Reading it, you won't be able to resist rededicating yourself to your practice. Lizos eliminates the uncertainty one often feels when approaching these traditions. He teaches us to show up respectfully, without appropriating, moving beyond a transactional relationship with the deities to one of reciprocity and care. You'll finish this book understanding the fundamentals of Greek magical practice, and what you learn might surprise you. Rather than the vindictive, petty deities often portrayed in popular mythology, we encounter the gods in their true form as inspirers, creators, and guides. After reading this book, you won't know how you were able to live without them."

—AMANDA YATES GARCIA, author of *Initiated: Memoir of a Witch* and host of *Between the Worlds* podcast

"*Secrets of Greek Mysticism* gives the reader beautiful and clear insights into the path of spirituality, communion, and connection with the Divine through ancient knowledge and wisdom that is needed in the world right now. George has created a beautiful flow throughout the book that really helps both beginners and more experienced spiritual seekers to cultivate a deeper practice with the different archetypes of the Divine and how to integrate them into our daily lives."

—SHEREEN OBERG, certified yoga and meditation teacher, creator of the *Law of Positivism* Instagram, and podcast, and author of *The Law of Positivism*

"*Secrets of Greek Mysticism* is a must-read for anyone looking to explore and deepen their connection with the ancient gods and goddesses. George Lizos brings ancient Greek wisdom and traditions into the present in an easy-to-understand, inclusive, and practical way for both those new to the path and modern mystics looking to go deeper with their practices. Featuring a wealth of information about working with the gods and goddesses as well as rituals and grounded advice, *Secrets of Greek Mysticism* is a must-have for any true seeker's bookshelf."

—VICTORIA MAXWELL, bestselling author of *Witch, Please* and *Manifest Your Dreams*

"In *Secrets of Greek Mysticism,* George shows us how ancient deities become guides for creating magic in everyday life. George's insightful exploration of Hellenic spirituality offers a fresh perspective, going beyond mythology to reveal the gods and goddesses as embodiments of qualities relevant to our modern world. Through practical exercises, rituals, and thought-provoking insights, George encourages readers to connect with the divine energies of the gods and integrate their transformative qualities into their personal and spiritual journeys."

>—EMMA MUMFORD, manifestation expert and bestselling author of *Hurt, Healing, Healed* and *Positively Wealthy*

"*Secrets of Greek Mysticism* is a wonderful book that allows you to put the power of the Greek gods and goddesses into your life in applicable and practical ways, while honoring their wisdom and magic!"

>—SAHARA ROSE, bestselling author of *Discover Your Dharma* and host of *Highest Self* Podcast

"*Secrets of Greek Mysticism* beautifully delves into the heart of ancient Greek spirituality, enlightening readers about the profound distinctions between myth and theology and providing a roadmap to work with the Greek gods for guidance and assistance in everyday life."

>—TAMMY MASTROBERTE, bestselling author of *The Universe Is Talking to You*

"George Lizos reimagines the Greek pantheon, allowing readers to tap into their wisdom in meaningful ways. With practical exercises and profound insights, this book opens a gateway to a deeper understanding of the divine energies that have shaped the foundations of Greek spirituality."

>—ANANTA RIPA AJMERA, bestselling author of *The Way of the Goddess*

"Through *Secrets of Greek Mysticism,* George Lizos invites us to embrace the divine energies of the Greek pantheon, providing a practical guide to incorporating their virtues into modern life. George's extensive knowledge as a spiritual teacher and priest shines through as he weaves together historical context, personal anecdotes, and guided practices to deepen our relationship with the deities. This book not only enriches our understanding of Hellenic spirituality but also empowers us to engage with spirit on a personal level, cultivating a harmonious union between ancient wisdom and contemporary living."

>—AMY LEIGH MERCREE, medical intuitive and bestselling author of eighteen books including *Aura Alchemy*

"*Secrets of Greek Mysticism* is a beautiful book that takes us deep into the mysteries, wonder, and power of the Greek gods and goddesses. In doing so, it sparks a journey of spiritual discovery through the lens of this incredible pantheon. George's unique background as a priest infuses so much authenticity and depth into his words, and it will help readers connect with the divine ancient Greek energies and how they can richly impact our modern lives today."

> —JULIE PARKER, priestess, sacred leadership mentor, and bestselling author of *Priestess*

"*Secrets of Greek Mysticism* has brought the gods and goddesses of Olympus alive. There are powerful activations embedded in George's personal stories of meeting the deities and also within the rituals. This book is more than just learning about the archetypes; it teaches us how to navigate our ascension process as a soul. The detailed way that George explains our connection to the universe and the divine purpose of oneself is enlightening and easy to understand. Anyone who is looking for a deeper spiritual practice with the Greek gods and goddesses will find answers in this book."

> —PAMELA CHEN, author and creator of *Enchanted Crystal Magic*, *The Mandarin Tree*, *Witchling Academy Tarot*, and *Tarot of the Owls*

"The Greek gods and goddesses are the foundation of Western civilization and have always been a great wonder for me. George offers his wisdom through his kind, heartfelt, and cheerful personality. *Secrets of Greek Mysticism* is a must-read for anyone interested in their own inner healing."

> —ANJIE CHO, feng shui educator and author of *Mindful Homes* and *Holistic Spaces*

"An indispensable guide to the heart of Greek spirituality, *Secrets of Greek Mysticism* expertly presents theology and practices that allow us to embody the virtues of the gods. Through the richly woven chapters, readers are guided to embrace the gods, not as distant figures but as companions on their spiritual path."

> —DANIELLE PAIGE, intuitive astrologer and spiritual teacher

"*Secrets of Greek Mysticism* is the book I have been waiting for! George takes the mythos and reminds us of the true magic it always was; is. I am a huge fan of Greek mythology; now I can really see how the gods and goddesses can be used in a practical way to help with self-discovery and growth. Ritual, meditation, and mantras bring even more vibrancy, and I cannot wait to get started on implementing them! Thank you for writing this, George."

> —DAVID WELLS, astrologer, past-life therapist, and creator of *The Tree of Life Oracle*

"George masterfully weaves ancient wisdom with modern insight, bringing the Greek pantheon to life in a way that's both accessible and deeply inspiring. Whether you're new to these deities or a devoted follower, this book offers a captivating journey to connect with Higher Power."

—CAEL O'DONNELL, psychic medium and author of *Three Minutes with Spirit*

"George achieves something truly divine with his work in *Secrets of Greek Mysticism*. He illuminates that mythology is not merely for study; it is a vibrant practice to be lived, inviting us to expect and embrace results as magnificent and profound as those experienced by the Gods themselves."

—SERGIO MAGAÑA, author of *The Toltec Secret, The Real Toltec Prophecies,* and *Caves of Power*

Secrets *of* Greek Mysticism

Secrets *of* Greek Mysticism

A MODERN GUIDE TO DAILY PRACTICE
WITH THE GREEK GODS AND GODDESSES

GEORGE LIZOS

HAMPTON ROADS

This edition first published in 2024 by Hampton Roads Publishing, an imprint of
Red Wheel/Weiser, LLC
With offices at:
65 Parker Street, Suite 7
Newburyport, MA 01950

Sign up for our newsletter and special offers by going to *www.redwheelweiser.com/newsletter*

Cover design by Brittany Craig
Cover art, *Entanglement of Past, Present, Future* © Mike Willcox
Moon images on pages 209 and 213 by saemilee/iStock. All other interior images by
    Century Library/Creative Market.
Interior by Happenstance Type-O-Rama
Typeset in Arno Pro, Berkeley Old Style, and Futura PT

ISBN: 978-1-64297-052-4

Library of Congress Cataloging-in-Publication Data available upon request.

Printed in the United States of America
IBI

10 9 8 7 6 5 4 3 2 1

For Vlassis Rassias

TABLE OF CONTENTS

PART III: Connecting *with the* Gods

PROLOGUE

"Let's go on a temple-hopping trip to Greece!" I cried out excitedly. Sargis, my best friend, stared at me with a puzzled look, wondering what on Earth I was talking about. "You know how college students go bar- or club-hopping? We'll go temple-hopping," I said matter-of-factly. He squinted his eyes curiously, prompting me to elaborate. I went on to explain the detailed plan I'd spent the past few weeks devising and researching.

Three years before, in 2017, I'd traveled to Athens to complete a priesthood training in Greek Polytheism, the indigenous, pagan religion of the ancient Greeks. By that point, my spiritual journey had led me to a number of spiritual practices and traditions, but nothing felt quite like home. It wasn't until a spiritual epiphany in Glastonbury, UK (which you can read about in my book *Lightworkers Gotta Work*), that I was guided to reconnect with the Earth-based spiritual traditions of my ancestors.

Having completed my practical training, I was hungry for knowledge. We all have strong energetic bonds or cords connecting us to the spirituality of our ancestors. When we reactivate them, they almost take over our entire being and guide our path. It's as if our ancestors are desperately waiting for us to wake up and remember them; and, once we do, they don't miss an opportunity to step in and impart their wisdom.

Consequently, for the previous three years I'd been obsessing over ancient Greek spirituality. I had been reading books on Greek religion and philosophy, attending workshops, performing rituals, and having deep conversations with my pagan friends. I particularly enjoyed getting to know and connecting with the Greek gods and goddesses, and I craved deeper connection with them.

It didn't take me long to realize that most of what I was taught about Greek religion and the gods and goddesses throughout my life had been completely false, even fabricated. I'd grown up believing that the ancient Greeks prayed to lifeless idols, that the gods and goddesses were simply mythological characters. Moreover, any mention of a Greek religion and the way it was erased by the early Christians was omitted from history books; hence, my understanding of my ancestors' traditions was very limited, to say the least.

While I quenched my thirst for knowledge with books, I yearned to know the gods in a deeper and more palpable way. I'd loved exploring, meditating, and learning about and performing rituals at the few ancient Greek and Roman temples in Cyprus—namely, the temples to Apollo and Aphrodite—but there were so many more gods and goddesses I wanted to connect with. So, a temple-hopping trip seemed the best way forward.

On March 3, 2020 (right when the COVID-19 pandemic hit Greece!), Sargis and I flew to Athens, and from there we toured central Greece and visited more than 15 ancient temples. We started by visiting Athena, Ares, and Hephaestus at the Athens Acropolis and Agora, made our way to Cape Sounion to pay our respects to Poseidon, traveled north to Delphi to connect with Apollo, went to Epidaurus to journey with Artemis and Asclepius, fell in love with Hera in Argos, and praised Zeus at Olympia, among others.

Thinking ahead and knowing that I'd eventually want to write a book about the Greek gods and goddesses, I created a plan to make the most out of the trip. At each temple we visited, we'd make an offering to the gods, use my dowsing rods to find the best place to meditate, and then journal about our insights. As a result, by the end of the trip I had a journal full of notes and guidance, which I consulted while writing this book.

In the years that followed, I kept deepening my connection with the gods through daily ritual and supplemented that with further reading and training. Therefore, the book you have in your hands is the culmination of a lifelong spiritual journey of searching, yearning for, and finally embracing my roots, stepping into my authenticity, and unlocking the secrets of the ancient Greeks. It's an honor to share this information with you, and I hope it serves you well on your journey.

INTRODUCTION

All the answers we seek are found in nature. I believe this with all my heart. Even before I became interested in Earth-based spirituality, I found myself searching for answers in nature. In my early childhood, while other kids would play video games or hang out at the latest cool spot downtown, I'd hang out in garden centers with my mum. I loved being surrounded by so many different plants and flowers, and I'd spend hours observing and learning about them. In my teenage years, I'd come home after a brutal day of getting bullied and rush to an acacia tree near my house. I'd find shelter under the embrace of its thick foliage and let it transmute my pain. When it was time to go to college, I chose to study geography and spent three years learning about rivers, glaciers, and volcanoes.

It was during college that I was awakened to the power and wisdom of the Earth, which eventually led me to explore Earth-based spirituality. The Earth is 4.543 billion years old, while the human race is approximately 200,000 years old—a tiny fraction of time in relation to the Earth's age. Over the course of its existence, the Earth has utilized powerful practices to maintain her vitality. Through earthquakes, hurricanes, ocean currents, atmospheric systems, and volcanic eruptions, she has systematically flushed out impurities and sustained her balance.

The ancient Greeks and other ancient civilizations knew this about the Earth, and rather than impose their rule on her they partnered and peacefully coexisted with her. They respected and took care of her, studied and learned from her processes, and aligned their lives with her rhythms. The Earth in turn showered them with her magic and wisdom, which allowed them to ascend spiritually, expand human consciousness, and create one of the world's greatest civilizations.

The legacy of the ancient Greeks includes the conception of democracy, philosophy, and the theater; significant advances in art, architecture, science, medicine, and technology; and much more. But while their legacy in terms of these contributions is well established, their spirituality and religious beliefs have been demoted to mythology and idolatry. We've been taught that the gods and goddesses were cruel and punishing figures the Greeks made up, that Greek myths were simply products of people's wild imaginations, and that Greek religion was just a series of transactional practices with no real substance. Is it possible that a culture that produced some of the Western world's greatest artists, scientists, and philosophers could have gotten religion so wrong? Or is something else at play here?

In this book, I pull back the curtain and share with you the truth about Greek spirituality, religion, and gods and goddesses. Whether you're a practicing pagan, witch, or lightworker, or you're just interested in learning about the ancient Greeks or Earth-based spirituality, this book will give you a solid foundation in Greek mysticism that you can use to deepen your practice.

How to Read This Book

My work has always revolved around helping lightworkers and spiritual seekers to find, follow, and fulfill their life purpose. *Secrets of Greek Mysticism* presents a complete system with step-by-step practices, rituals, meditations, and activations to help you do so.

The book is divided into three parts that build on one another, so I suggest that you read it sequentially. However, you may also use it as a reference guide to quickly find specific information about Greek spirituality, the gods and goddesses, and ritual practices.

Here's what you can expect to learn in each part:

- **Part I: The Nature of the Gods** provides you with a foundation in ancient Greek spirituality, cosmology, and theology. This is an essential step to learning about the true nature of the gods, as opposed to the reductive, mythological perception of them we so often encounter. By the end of this part, you'll understand how mythology and theology differ; the nature of the Universe, the cosmos, and the gods; the soul's journey of ascension; and how you can use this information to progress on your spiritual path.

- **Part II: Getting to Know the Gods** introduces the 12 Olympian gods. Each chapter has a set structure, discussing the god's essence and virtues, while providing an ascension toolkit with a mantra, journal prompts, symbols, hymns, practices, and activations to help you connect with the gods.

- **Part III: Connecting with the Gods** shares ways of working with the gods and goddesses on a daily, monthly, and yearly basis. This part starts with a framework using the Greek Wheel of the Year. It then offers guidance on setting up altars; includes scripts on performing new moon, full moon, and other rituals.

Since this is a practical book, on many occasions I'll ask you to write things down. As a result, it'll be beneficial to have a journal dedicated to this journey. Whether it is an electronic or a physical one, keeping all the processes in one place will help you keep track of your progress and revisit the practices when you need to.

We're in This Together

I'm fully committed to helping you get to the finish line, and I want to be there for you every step of the way. Here's what you can do to help me support you on this journey:

- **Join my private Facebook Group community, *Your Spiritual Toolkit*.** This is a safe and supportive community of like-minded people who are all on this journey with you. Use this group to ask questions, contribute your answers, and share your journey through the book. I'm actively involved in the group, and I'll be there to cheer you on along the way.

- **Follow me on Instagram (@georgelizos) and keep me posted on your progress.** Send me DMs and tag me in your posts and stories using the hashtag #SecretsOfGreekMysticism. I read all of my comments and messages and personally reply to everything.

- **Download the *Secrets of Greek Mysticism* resources** at *www.GeorgeLizos .com/SOGM*. These include extra content that I haven't included in the book, information sheets for each god, cheat sheets, checklists, and downloadable guided mediations of the gods' activations.

I look forward to hearing from you and supporting you along your journey. I have every confidence in you, and I can't wait to see you live your most divinely guided life.

PART I

The Nature
of the
Gods

CHAPTER 1

Types of Religions

To fully and properly understand the nature of the Greek gods, it's important that you also understand the religious context in which they were created and venerated. Therefore, we'll start your journey of ascending with the gods by first setting a strong foundation of Greek theology and cosmology.

In this chapter, I'll introduce the nature and characteristics of Greek paganism in relation to modern religions.

Two Types of Religions

When you look at the history of religions and spiritual traditions across the millennia, you'll identify two main types of religions:

- **Natural or Earth-based religions.** The first type are the natural, Earth-based religions, also known as pagan religions. Examples of natural religions include all the indigenous and ethnic religions of different cultures. For example, Greek paganism is the natural, ethnic religion of the ancient Greek world, Hinduism is a Desi natural religion, Celtic paganism is the ancient religion of the Celtic people in Europe, and Shinto is a natural Japanese religion. There are thousands of natural religions— some of them widespread, and others limited to specific regions, towns, or villages.

Natural religions developed as a result of humans' observation of and relationship with the Earth and the cosmos. They're called *natural* religions partly because they're inseparably connected with the rhythms and cycles of nature and the laws of the Universe, but also because they developed organically from people's interactions with the natural world. Thus, natural religions are philosophical religions. They developed as a result of humans' progressive understanding of the divine through communication (*logos*), philosophy, and observation.

Another important characteristic of natural religions is that they acknowledge and honor religious diversity. Since natural religions are intrinsically tied to the land and the people who created them, they accept other religions and spiritual traditions as natural expressions of different people's idiosyncrasies. Therefore, there's no need or desire to expand into new territories or assert their dominance over other religions, and they accept other cultures' religions as their unique understanding of the divine.

• **Founded religions.** The second type of religions are the founded ones. These started developing approximately 2,500 years ago, and they're usually based on the religious perspectives and worldviews of the person who founded them. Examples of founded religions are the Abrahamic religions, such as Judaism, Christianity, and Islam. The most distinctive characteristic of founded religions is that they attempt to shape the world according to their founder's beliefs based on the premise that their founder had a divine revelation, is a messenger of god, or sees themselves as god incarnate.

Founded religions are dogmatic and consider their understanding of the divine and the world as the only and absolute truth. As a result, they seek to expand their dominance over other religions, often employing violence to do so. A quick look at the history of most natural religions reveals that their decline has been the result of systematic violence, brutality, and persecution by founded religions.

The Resurgence of Earth-Based Spirituality

As a result of religious freedom and the proliferation of knowledge in many parts of the world, there has been a resurgence of Earth-based spirituality. Natural religions are no longer solely tied to the countries, cultures, and idiosyncrasies of the people who created them. Instead, New Ageism and neopaganism have led to the blending of various indigenous spiritual traditions to create new ways of honoring and working with the Earth's cycles. Popular neopagan religions include Wicca, neo-druidry, the Goddess movement, and eclectic paganism.

Centered around a respect of the Earth and a desire to work with the natural laws of the Universe to create positive change, modern pagan traditions usually bring together spiritual practices and deities from various natural religions. This form of syncretism also took place during ancient times, when physically or culturally neighboring cultures would adopt practices or merge similar gods into unified deities. However, although ancient syncretism was gradual and based on spiritual similarities between deities and practices, neopagan syncretism sometimes waters down the true meaning of the original practices for the sake of simplification, commercialization, or merely the creation of something new.

As a result, many of the deeper messages and meanings behind Earth-based religions and their various gods and goddesses stay hidden and are instead replaced by shallow practices and reductive symbolic representations. For example, the descriptions of most pagan gods and goddesses in New Age and neopagan books stick to the mythological characteristics of these deities without making an effort to reveal their full essence. Aphrodite is limited to being a goddess of love, sex, and beauty, rather than the creative force of nature that she truly is. Ares is condemned as a violent war god due to his mythological representation, which completely disregards the qualities of courage and tenacity that his essence truly evokes.

To wholly understand the nature of the Greek gods, and natural religions in general, we need to study them as part of the spiritual and cultural context in which they were created and learn from the indigenous people who practiced them in the past and still do today. Only then can we truly understand their essence and receive their wisdom. Doing so not only is respectful to these natural religions but also allows you to create a deeper and more meaningful personal, eclectic syncretism if you so choose.

New Age practices have often been criticized for appropriating and oversimplifying indigenous religions. Although this is true in many ways, it's also important to understand that we're all unique human beings who deserve to find our own path for working with the divine, even if that means combining different spiritual practices.

Having been a New Ager for many years myself, I've found the balance between syncretism and appropriation by taking the time to properly understand, read about, and honor the cultures and traditions behind the practices I use.

Although I am a practicing Greek pagan priest, my aim is not to convert you to Greek paganism (as discussed, this goes against the very essence of natural religions), nor to discourage you from merging spiritual practices and deities of different spiritual traditions. Instead, my goal in writing this book is to provide you with a solid foundation of Greek paganism and an understanding of the 12 main gods so that you can honor the religion while also using this knowledge to craft your own personalized spiritual practice.

CHAPTER 2

The Universe and the Cosmos

T he Greek gods and goddesses are intimately tied to the Universe and the cosmos. In this chapter, we'll continue our exploration of Greek religion by examining the differences between and relationship of the Universe and the cosmos.

The Universe

The Universe has had many names through the years. It's been referred to as God, the Creator, Spirit, Source, Infinite Intelligence, the All, or—as the ancient Greeks referred to it—True Being. In this book I'll refer to it as the Universe, but feel free to think of it in the way that makes the most sense to you.

To understand what the Universe is, we first need to accept that it's impossible to do so fully from within our limited human perspective. Although we're physical extensions of the Universe, we're limited by our physicality and can only fully understand its nature when we've transitioned back to it. Instead, we can make educated guesses, which is what humans have done since the dawn of time.

According to ancient Greek spirituality, the Universe has four main characteristics:

- **The Universe is absolute.** The Universe is all that is. There's nothing outside of it; otherwise, it wouldn't be the All. This means that the cosmos and anything that's beyond it—in all dimensions, and across time and space—are all part of the Universe. Anything you can think of, or cannot think of because you're not aware of, is part of the Universe.

- **The Universe is infinite.** Since there's nothing outside of the Universe, there's nothing to define, confine, or limit its boundaries. It's in a constant state of expansion in time and space. Being infinite and all that is, ever was, and ever will be, the Universe was never created and has always continuously existed. There was no beginning and no ending: if there were one, the force that created or ended it would be above it, and that's not possible.

- **The Universe is unchangeable.** The substance of the Universe is immutable. It cannot change in its true nature; it's perfect the way it is, and there's nothing to change or improve on. What we perceive as change is simply the constant evolution and expression of the Universe in different forms, states, and energies.

- **The Universe is loving.** The Universe is made up of love and light, quite literally. At the core of every physical manifestation within the Universe is the energy and vibration of love. There's no source of evil within the Universe, and the evils we encounter in the cosmos are simply manifestations of our disconnection from the Universe's ever-flowing love.

Every single piece of consciousness within the Universe, including ourselves and life as we know it, shares the Universe's absolute, infinite, unchangeable, and loving qualities. If we didn't share these characteristics, then we wouldn't be part of the Universe, and that cannot be because there's nothing outside the Universe.

The Cosmos

The physical universe (not to be confused with the Universe, meaning Source) or, as the ancient Greeks referred to it, the *cosmos*, is a manifestation and thus an extension of the Universe (Source) in physical form. In Greek the word *cosmos* means jewel and adornment, as the cosmos is the part of the Universe that has acquired natural order and attained harmony and beauty. The few remaining parts of the cosmos are referred to as *Tartarus*, which derives from the Greek word *tarachē*, meaning disorder. These are the parts of the Universe, outside of the cosmos, whose qualities haven't yet been defined.

You can think of the cosmos as being divided into two levels: one that's eternal and one that's perishable. The eternal level of the cosmos consists of the invisible substance that makes up its essence, the infinite intelligence and divine life-force energy that flows through and powers all life. At this level, the cosmos maintains the Universe's qualities of being absolute, infinite, and unchangeable. Thus, it was never created and cannot be destroyed. Instead, its internal order arose naturally through a never-ending process of emergence or arising, as each one of its forms emerged through the previous one.

CHAPTER 3

The Gods and Goddesses

Having discussed the nature of Greek paganism and explored the relationship between the Universe and the cosmos, we'll now focus exclusively on the gods and goddesses and see how they fit into this cosmological system.

Characteristics of the Gods

The gods and goddesses are extensions and mirrors of the Universe. They're the Universe multiplied into separate beings, which are also still part of the whole. Rather than simply being energies, deities, or archetypes that form part of the Universe like most other spirit guides, the gods and goddesses *are* the Universe. They share the Universe's qualities, embody Universal laws and functions (to which they're also subject), and share the Universe's mission to create and sustain harmony and order in the cosmos.

Specifically, the gods share the following characteristics:

- **They're loving.** As extensions of the Universe, the gods share the Universe's qualities of purity and loveliness. In contrast to their portrayal in myths (see Chapter 4 for more about mythology), they're free from human passions and have no malice. There's nothing evil or mean-spirited about them, and their common purpose is to uphold the Universal laws they represent and ensure the smooth running and evolution of the cosmos.

- **They're unchangeable.** The gods are as immutable as the Universe and the cosmos. Any change we perceive in the cosmos is simply the recycling of energy, but the essence of all things remains constant. If the gods, the cosmos, and the Universe were to change in any way, that would imply a change to love or fear, good or bad, better or worse. This simply cannot be; otherwise, the Universe wouldn't be the All, and the gods wouldn't be its true representations.

- **They're eternal.** Since the Universe has always existed, so have the gods. They're extensions of the primary essence of creation; therefore, they were never born and cannot die. Instead, they evolve and express in different ways, like the Universe does and has done for eternity.

- **They don't have a physical body.** Physical bodies come with limitations and constraints; therefore, the gods cannot have a physical body. However, as extensions of the Universe they automatically exist within all bodies, including humans. In other words, the gods live within us at all times, and it's up to us to tune in to their presence and receive their wisdom.

- **They're not confined by physical space.** Similarly, the gods cannot be confined within a specific physical space, as that would imply their separation from the Universe. Instead, the gods exist everywhere and at all times. They're the divine substance that flows through everyone and everything and keeps the world running.

Types of Gods

There are thousands of gods and goddesses, as many as there are Universal laws and functions. As explained by Neoplatonic author Salutius (355–367 AD), the gods can be divided into two main types: cosmic and hypercosmic. As their name suggests, the cosmic gods create and run the cosmos, while the hypercosmic gods dwell in the creation of mind, soul, and spirit. The gods we're most interested in connecting with are the cosmic ones—specifically, the 12 main gods of Olympus.

The reason these 12 gods have been venerated more than other gods isn't a matter of chance but instead a matter of order. Specifically, the cosmic gods are divided into four main orders: those who create the world, those who animate it, those who harmonize it, and those who maintain that harmony. All of these tasks have a beginning, middle, and end, each of which is governed by a god of Olympus. Therefore, there are 12 main gods that govern our world and the cosmos:[1]

Creation: Zeus, Poseidon, Hephaestus

Animation: Demeter, Hera, Artemis

Harmonization: Apollo, Aphrodite, Hermes

Maintenance: Hestia, Athena, Ares

You can easily spot the primary purposes of the Olympian gods through the ways they have been depicted in art over the years, as well as in their various myths. For example, Zeus is presented holding a thunderbolt (which symbolizes the life-force energy that creates the cosmos), Artemis is depicted with a bow and a deer (symbolic of the animism of the cosmos), Apollo is often portrayed tuning a lyre (because he's harmonizing the world), and Athena is often armed (to maintain and protect the order of the cosmos).

These four tasks or purposes are the gods' powers, their spheres of influence when it comes to the cosmos. They're also the four main pillars of manifestation, which are innate to how the Universe, the cosmos, and we create life and expand human consciousness. Think about your personal journey of manifesting anything, in all areas of your life. First you come up with an idea or a desire (creation); then, you put in the work to manifest it (animation). Following that, you fine-tune and perfect your creation as it comes to life (harmonization); finally, you maintain what you've created (maintenance) and build upon it by coming up with a new desire and going through the cycle once again.

This four-step cycle is the rhythm of the cosmos and everything it contains, including ourselves. Not only do the gods run this primordial process, they actually *are* the process. Therefore, anything that's manifested, and everything that is, has been created, animated, harmonized, and maintained by the 12 gods—the 12 main functions of the Universe.

Beyond the 12 main Olympian gods, there are subsidiary gods representing minor Universal laws, functions, and processes, all working within an Olympian's sphere of influence. For example, healing god Asclepius is contained within Apollo, the Three Graces within Aphrodite, Dionysus within Zeus, and Pan within Dionysus.

Why We Pray to the Gods

A widespread misconception about the ancient Greeks is that they had a transactional relationship with the gods. Even scholars who have dedicated their lives to researching the ancient Greeks get it all wrong, teaching that the Greeks prayed and sacrificed to the gods in order to appease them or gain their favor. This misconception is largely based on the misinterpreted mythological perspective of the gods having human passions, spreading fear, and imposing their will on human life. This perception couldn't be further from the truth!

The gods don't need prayers or offerings, nor do they favor or punish us in any way. Being pure and unchangeable, the gods can't feel positive or negative about our actions, as feeling either way would go against their neutral essence. Consequently, it's illogical to assume that the divine is affected in any way by human actions and hence that they need to be appeased, since there's no favor to be gained. They love and favor us by default, because this is their true and only nature.

When we are and do good, we're in alignment with the gods and able to feel their light shining upon us. When our actions aren't aligned with the gods' love and purity, then we cannot feel the gods' presence within and around us. The gods don't become our enemies; rather, we become our own enemies by preventing ourselves from receiving their love and light. The favors or punishments that we perceive the gods give us, then, are favors and punishments we give to ourselves as a result of our misalignment from the gods and therefore our own, true essence.

Prayers or offerings are simply ways to symbolically reach out to the gods in an effort to regain our alignment with them through self-forgiveness or to simply deepen our state of alignment. In other words, the gods don't need the prayers and offerings—we do. The gods gain nothing from our prayers or offerings because they're already pure, absolute, and unchangeable in their essence and the way they perceive us. On the other hand, we have a lot to gain through these actions, especially when we do them with the intention of living in alignment with the gods' essence and purpose.

When you look at the ways in which the ancient Greeks worshiped the gods, as well as the methods of veneration for most religions and spiritual traditions, you'll notice there's a symbolic element. This symbolism is centered around creating sacred space—that is, giving the divine a more physical presence so that we can feel closer to it. In the case of the ancient Greeks, the temples symbolized the Universe, the altar stood for the Earth, and the gods' statues were lifelike so that humans could feel closer to and see themselves in them. The hymns and prayers symbolized thought, and the offerings physical matter.

Masculine and Feminine Gods

Although we portray the gods in binary human genders, they're really genderless. As I explained in the previous section, the reason we've historically portrayed the gods in human, lifelike statues is so that we could feel closer to them. Many religions and spiritual traditions have done and still do this, as it's an easy way to make the invisible visible and bring the sacred into the profane world.

From a spiritual standpoint, since the gods are Universal laws, energies, and functions, they don't really have a physical form, name, or gender. Humans ascribed their forms, names, and genders in their desire to better understand and connect with the gods. This is why pagan gods share similar characteristics across the various pagan traditions: Greek goddess Aphrodite is similar to the Mesopotamian goddess Ishtar, Apollo shares similar characteristics with the Egyptian god Ra, and Zeus shares similarities with the Norse Thor. In essence, each ancient culture ascribed the same Universal functions different forms, names, genders, and characteristics according to its understanding of the cosmos and the Universe.

Greek gods' genders were usually given as a result of the gods' dominant energy in relation to their unique Universal functions and qualities. To better understand this, let's consider the differences between masculine and feminine energy.

> *Gender is in everything; everything has its masculine*
> *and feminine principles; Gender manifests on all planes.*
>
> —*THE KYBALION*

Ontologically, everything in the cosmos and the Universe manifests as a result of the interaction between Divine Masculine and Divine Feminine energy. These energies are different from the biological sex (male/female/intersex), or social gender (man/woman/nonbinary). Instead, they're the two primordial energies that are involved in the creation of all things.

A prime example of how masculine and feminine energies drive the manifestation process is the way in which atoms are formed. Essentially, atoms are created when a positive ion (masculine energy) exerts influence on a negative ion (feminine energy). Since atoms are the physical makeup of everything on the physical plane, then all creation—whether it's on the physical, mental, or spiritual plane—is the result of the interplay of, and is balanced in, masculine and feminine energy.

The Divine Masculine energy directs and expresses energy, starting the creative process and seeing things to completion. It creates a framework and a plan, directing the action required for things to manifest. Masculine energy is like a project manager, choosing the right team and materials, handing out responsibilities, and orchestrating the manifestation process.

On the other hand, the Divine Feminine energy receives instructions, makes sense of them, creates space for manifestation, and does the generating work of bringing the manifestations to life. Simply put, masculine energy directs creation, and feminine energy is the womb that births those creative manifestations into the world.

From this perspective, the masculine and feminine gods were given their respective genders according to the primary energy they possess. This doesn't mean that masculine gods don't have feminine qualities, or vice versa; it simply means that their energy is primarily masculine or feminine. Concurrently, although the gods were given a gender they were also simultaneously balanced in both masculine and feminine energies—that is, there's feminine in the masculine, and masculine in the feminine. These primordial energies aren't mutually exclusive but rather two sides of the same coin.

In fact, the gods have often been portrayed with both genders to demonstrate their balanced nature. For example, Aphrodite's male version is Aphroditus, Zeus's female version is Dione, and the moon goddess Selene was often also honored as the male god Men. The balanced masculine/feminine energy is also present in a number of intersex gods whose Universal qualities and energies ascribed them a more fluid depiction. Examples of intersex gods include Hermaphroditus, the offspring of Hermes and Aphrodite; Agdistis, who possessed both male and female genitalia; Phanes, a deity of procreation and the generation of new life; and the Naiad nymph Salmacis, among many others.

Additionally, in early antiquity, before the glorious temples and imposing statues, the ancient Greeks depicted gods as blocks of wood, stones, pillars, or simply trees, without any anthropomorphic characteristics or genders. This demonstrates their understanding of the nonbinary nature of the gods, and it also frees us to depict, name, and honor the gods in whatever way makes sense to us.

There Are No Evil Gods

Another misconception about the Greek gods, and pagan gods in general, is that they're of evil or demonic nature. This misconception was largely created by early Christians in their successful attempt to suppress the Old Religion and replace it with the new one.

In spiritual truth, there are no evil or demonic gods. To begin with, the term *demon*, or *daimon* in Greek, had nothing to do with evil spirits in the ancient world. Instead, daimons were loving and protective beings of light, very similar to what we call angels today. More specifically, according to the Orphics, as we ascend in our spiritual journeys over multiple incarnations, we eventually evolve from humans to heroes to daimons, and then we enter the realm of the gods.

What we understand today as evil spirits or demonic entities are etheric manifestations of the disconnection from the gods' love and light. Since the gods are extensions of the Universe, and the Universe is pure and loving, there can't be a source of evil, as it would have to be contained within the Universe. If there were a source of evil, then the gods and the Universe wouldn't be pure and loving. Thus, since the gods and the Universe *are* pure and loving, evil spirits or acts are the results of people's misalignment from the gods and their pure and loving nature.

In my book *Protect Your Light*, I talk about *collective thought forms*. These are vibrational clouds that contain the collective thoughts, emotions, and energy of fears and limiting beliefs. They're created when many people think and feel the same low-vibrational thoughts and emotions for a sustained period of time. The vibration of their thoughts and emotions coalesces into these collective thought forms.

This is the process through which evil spirits and demonic entities are also created. Although it's true that these manifestations exist within the realm of the gods, they're not *of* the gods. There's no source of evil from which they draw their power, no devil to take instructions from. They're beingless etheric manifestations that we've created as a result of our own distance from the gods' and our own true essence and vibration.

CHAPTER 4

Mythology vs. Theology

Most misconceptions about the Greek gods are a result of their mythology. The early Christians were so successful in burying and distorting the truth and essence of the Old Religion that most people still believe that the Greek gods are simply products of fictitious myths and that the ancient Greeks prayed to lifeless idols. As a result, the Greek gods are thought of as violent and full of human passions, in contrast to the supposed purity and love of the Christian God. This is untrue.

The most important thing to understand about mythology is that it's different from theology. Theology is the study of the gods and religious practices, while mythology is an allegorical collection of stories that draw from theology in an effort to communicate the gods' qualities in both an educational and entertaining way. In other words, mythology draws from theology, but theology doesn't draw from mythology. Therefore, the myths are subject to symbolic interpretation and deliberation, and are not to be taken literally.

Often, the myths were created by deeply spiritual and religious people in an effort to convey multilayered meanings of and messages from the gods. Certain information in the myths could be understood by everyone, while high-level concepts could be interpreted only by those who studied the nature of the gods and the Universe, such as the students of mystery schools. The myths were meant to make people think outside the box and search for deeper spiritual meanings, which they could use to get closer to the gods and progress on their spiritual journeys. Thus, you could think of the myths as didactic spiritual tools for ascension.

Let's consider the myth of the Golden Apple of Discord, which is said to have led to the Trojan War. As the myth goes, during a feast of the gods at the wedding of Peleus and Thetis, Eris, the goddess of discord, tossed a golden apple as a prize for the most beautiful goddess. This ignited a vanity-fueled quarrel among Hera, Athena, and Aphrodite. The three goddesses agreed to Zeus's suggestion to let Paris of Troy choose the fairest one, and Paris chose Aphrodite.

In a first-level, literal interpretation, you see gods that compete, feel jealousy and resentment, and get caught up in a childish fight about who's prettier. When you interpret this myth from a symbolic and theological perspective, however, you see something completely different. The gods feasting together stands for their hyper-cosmic powers and their involvement in the creation and running of the cosmos. The golden apple that's thrown by the goddess Eris symbolizes the world, which is created out of opposites (the Divine Masculine and the Divine Feminine). The three goddesses' quarrel over the world signifies the various gifts and qualities that each goddess bestows upon it. Paris, being human and overpowered by his senses, can see only Aphrodite's obvious beauty and disregards the other goddesses' qualities; thus, he gives Aphrodite the apple.

You can now see the level of depth and meaning that's hidden within Greek myths, as well as the symbolic and contextual knowledge that's required to interpret them accurately. Unfortunately, much of the symbolism and deeper meanings have been lost over time, especially because the true meanings of the myths were rarely published; instead, they were kept secret by the various mystery schools of the time. Additionally, many of these myths have been changed over the years, which is why you should always take them with a grain of salt.

CHAPTER 5

Humans and the Gods

aving discussed the nested meaning of the Universe, the cosmos, and the gods, according to the ancient Greeks, we'll now talk about how *we* fit into the picture. We'll discuss the nature of mortal life and human beings, and how we relate to the gods, the cosmos, and the Universe.

Our Collective Purpose

To begin with, all mortal beings and things, whether humans, animals, plants, minerals, or inanimate physical objects, exist in two main planes of existence: the physical level of perishability and the immaterial level of spirit. The physical aspect of the mortal world dematerializes and transforms in an endless cycle of renewal, while the immaterial level of spirit and the soul is eternal and evolves and ascends through various incarnation cycles (more on this in Chapter 6).

Human beings specifically have evolved significantly through several incarnations so that we've activated *logos*, the capacity to think logically and acquire true knowledge. This differentiates us from other mortal beings because it enables us to organize ourselves in social groups, create laws and institutions, develop tools and skills, and, most importantly, expand consciousness through invention, civilization, and technology.

Our collective purpose as a human race is to preserve, perfect, and expand Universal consciousness. We're here to channel the energy and wisdom of the gods and the Universe to create more of life and contribute to the infinite expansion of the Universe. You can see the evidence of our collective purpose with a quick look at human history. We've evolved from living in caves and feeding on raw food to enjoying lavish lifestyles in megacities and relishing haute cuisine. The history of human race screams evolution, because this is what we're here to do.

Four Levels of Purpose

Drawing from our collective purpose, in my book *Lightworkers Gotta Work* I talk about our four levels of purpose, namely:

- **Collective purpose:** As discussed, our collective purpose is to expand Universal consciousness by perfecting our soul and the *cosmos*, therefore creating a more loving and kinder world.

- **Soul realm purpose:** *Soul realms* are groups of souls with a common purpose and characteristics. We all belong to a soul realm containing a blend of other realms, and our soul realm purpose draws from the collective purposes of our unique soul realm blend.

- **Soul purpose:** Our soul purpose draws from the collective soul realm purpose and consists of our soul's personal purpose fulfilled over several lives.

- **Life purpose:** Our personal life purpose draws from our soul purpose and has to do with fulfilling a specific mission as a step toward fulfilling our soul purpose.

From a human standpoint, our main concern is with identifying, following, and fulfilling our personal life purpose. This will allow us to progress along our soul's journey of ascension to fulfill our soul purpose as well as help us fulfill our soul realm and collective purposes of expanding the Universe and perfecting the cosmos.

Arete: Living a Virtuous Life

The process through which we follow and fulfill our four-tier purpose of perfecting ourselves and the world and ascending on our spiritual journey is known as *arete*, a

Greek word that translates to virtue, goodness, or excellence. *Arete* is the root of the English words *arithmetic* and *harmony*.

Arete was the foundation of Greek religion and formed part of a value system that consisted of dozens of virtues, acting as guideposts for living in accordance with the gods. Each god presides over certain virtues, and the goal was to understand and adopt these virtues in daily life. Doing so brought people closer to living life in the image of the gods, following their purpose, and therefore, ascending on their soul's journey.

Examples of these virtues include justice, courage, friendship, prudence, and magnanimity, all of which you can find woven into Greek myths, history, and philosophy. Although Greek religion never had a central book akin to the Christian Bible or the Islamic Koran, this ethical value system similarly guided them to living life in accordance with the gods.

In Part II of the book, you'll learn about the gods' various virtues in detail, as well as ways you can adopt them in your life, too.

CHAPTER 6

The Soul's Journey
of Ascension

Now we'll explore the journey of the soul from its creation to its spiritual ascension and beyond. This will further clarify our relationship with the gods, the cosmos, and the Universe, as well as light up the path to your spiritual journey of ascension.

Religion vs. Philosophy

Before we deep-dive into the journey of the soul, it's important to distinguish between ancient Greek religion and philosophy. In ancient times, Greek religion was primarily concerned with humans' lives from the moment they were born until the moment they died. Life before birth or after death wasn't the realm of religion but instead of philosophy. The prominent philosophical schools at the time were Platonism, Aristotelianism, Stoicism, Epicureanism, Pythagoreanism, and Orphism, most named for the philosophers who launched them.

Each philosophical school had different theories about the journey of the soul, and people were free to explore these theories and choose the one that most resonated with them. For example, whereas Platonism, Pythagoreanism, and Orphism ascribe to reincarnation, Stoicism and Epicureanism don't. They were all part of the central Greek religion, but they simply had different opinions about the nature and journey of the soul.

The philosophical schools I'm most in alignment with when it comes to the journey of the soul are the Platonic, Pythagorean, and (especially) Orphic, which are all quite similar. Therefore, the views I'll share in this chapter are largely based on these three schools. Interestingly, I'd already held these beliefs even before I converted to Greek Polytheism or knew about these schools. I was pleasantly surprised to discover that my beliefs on reincarnation and the journey of the soul—which I'd been teaching as part of my previous books, workshops, and private sessions—already aligned with these three philosophical schools.

I encourage you to have an open mind and let yourself consider the ideas I'm about to share, while also trusting your gut and forming your opinion on these matters. In other words, take what makes sense to you and let the rest go. Whether you accept, partly accept, or don't at all accept what I'm about to share, you'll still be able to connect with and work with the Greek gods in a powerful way.

The Journey of the Soul

Like everything else in the Universe, the soul is created as a result of the interaction between the two primordial, cosmogenic substances—the Divine Masculine and the Divine Feminine. According to the Law of Evolution, upon which all life is based, as soon as the soul is created it follows a journey of evolution or ascension.

As I explained earlier, the purpose of the soul's ascension journey is to perfect the cosmos and expand Universal consciousness, thereby creating more of life and making it better as well. To do so, the soul enters a developmental cycle of incarnations through which it has experiences, learns various lessons, and fulfills certain missions or purposes. According to the Orphics, the soul starts by incarnating as single-cell organisms and then ascends to the mineral, plant, and animal kingdoms. From there, it evolves to being human for many incarnations until it ascends beyond the physical plane and into the spiritual planes, to incarnate as a hero, a daimon, a god, an Olympian god, and beyond.

From this perspective, the soul's primary desire is to evolve from body to body across its cycle of incarnations, to learn lessons and fulfill various purposes, until it enters the higher planes of existence where true enlightenment is achieved. The soul acknowledges the importance of the material plane of existence as a necessary training ground for its spiritual evolution, but it's also mindful of not getting stuck—or, worse, regressing—in its evolutionary path. Spiritual regression happens when the soul fails to learn its chosen lessons or fulfill its purpose in a lifetime, which moves it backward in its developmental cycle and keeps it stuck in the material plane.

According to Orphism, then, the gods, including the Olympian gods, used to be humans who ascended through myriad incarnations until they transcended the physical realm, evolved in the spiritual realms, and gained Universal responsibilities. Souls that evolve to become a god take on one of the millions of Universal laws or functions to oversee, while they continue evolving to even higher realms of existence. Therefore, there's no end to spiritual ascension, and the soul's constantly on a journey of deeper enlightenment.

From this perspective, the evolution of the Universe, the cosmos, human souls, and the gods occurs simultaneously. The creation of the cosmos (cosmogenesis) leads to the creation and evolution of souls (psychogenesis), which in turn leads to the creation of the gods (theogenesis) and the expansion of the Universe.

The idea of humans evolving to be heroes, daimons, gods, and Olympian gods may seem a bit far-fetched at first. But this isn't too different from popular New Age theories (such as the Ascended Masters theory); the belief in incarnated angels, elementals, or starseeds; and the beliefs held by many other pagan traditions, particularly Eastern ones. This goes to show that New Age theories aren't really new at all, but instead really, really old.

CHAPTER 7

The Spiritual Meaning
of Olympus

A ccording to Greek mythology, the Olympian gods live in a palace at the peak of Mount Olympus in Greece. We've already discussed the allegorical significance of the myths, so what does Mount Olympus symbolize? Is it just an actual mountain peak that houses the energies of the gods, or is it something more?

The Four Planes of Existence

Every physical object in the cosmos has an energetic field, commonly known as the *aura*. The human aura, for example, has seven etheric layers that extend outward from the physical body and form an egglike shape around us. Each of these layers is a version of ourselves existing within a different dimension. Whereas our physical body exists in the third dimension, our etheric bodies exist in other dimensions that have their own rules, other beings, and energetic makeup.

Planet Earth as a whole also has various etheric layers that extend outward, beyond the moon and all the way to the sun. The Earth's aura is divided into four main levels, or planes of existence, each of which has different characteristics and is occupied by different beings:

- **The physical plane:** This primarily consists of physical matter, including solids, liquids, gases, ether (the medium that facilitates the transmission of information between matter and energy), and energy, which includes heat, light, magnetism, electricity, life force, and forms of energy that are not yet acknowledged by science and that the human mind can't yet fully comprehend.

- **The mental plane:** This is subdivided into the mineral, plant, elemental, animal, and human minds. The mineral, plant, and elemental minds correspond to the states and conditions of the elemental kingdoms and include fairies, gnomes, mermaids, and other types of elementals. The animal mind relates to the states and conditions of the world's animals, and the plane of the human mind comprises the states and conditions of humans.

- **The spiritual plane:** The third plane of existence consists of the plethora of spiritual beings, such as minor gods and goddesses, daimons, Ascended Masters, and other spirit guides. It's also the plane we have most access to, and communication with, when we connect to spirit in our spiritual practice.

- **The Olympian plane:** The fourth and final plane of existence has the highest frequency and is where the Olympian gods and other high-dimensional beings exist. Mount Olympus isn't just a physical mountain, then, but also a reference to the highest dimension of existence in the cosmos.

According to the Law of Correspondence, all four layers are interconnected, meaning that to some degree we can all access them to connect with, receive guidance from, and communicate with the beings in each plane. Your spiritual journey of ascension, then, is a journey up toward the four planes of existence through thousands of incarnations until you reach the Olympian plane.

Simultaneously, you can access the frequency of these planes in the here and now through your daily spiritual practice, in your connection with the gods, and by living in accordance to their virtues. Doing so keeps you connected to your true essence and purpose and provides you with moment-to-moment guidance to progress on your ascension journey.

PART II

Getting
to
Know
the
Gods

CHAPTER 8

Meditation Prep Process

I n the chapters of Parts II and III, I'll guide you through deep meditation journeys to meet the gods and goddesses, perform rituals, and receive intuitive guidance. I'll share about the gods in the order we celebrate them according to the Greek Wheel of the Year, starting in January and ending in December, as you'll read about in Chapter 22.

Before you do these meditations, it's important that you follow the three steps of relaxation, centering, and grounding, as described next. All three steps are of vital importance for both the effectiveness of the processes and your safety when practicing these meditations.

Relaxation

The most important factor for an effective meditation is that your mind and body are fully relaxed. The meditations you'll get to practice will take you on journeys to shift your energy, attune to spiritual frequencies, and interact with the gods and goddesses. This requires that you soften your physicality and allow your soul to take over, which is what conscious relaxation allows you to do.

Start by relaxing the top of your head and then progressively move all the way down to your feet. Don't rush the process, and instead focus on completely relaxing each part of your body—your eyes, cheeks, jaw, and so on.

As soon as you've reached the bottom of your feet, take three deep breaths in and, as you exhale, visualize that you're becoming a wet noodle. This is a great way to help you release any remaining tension from your physical body and allow you to let go completely.

Having relaxed your body, focus on relaxing your mind next. Although it won't be easy to fully empty your mind of thoughts, you can give it something small and insignificant to focus on instead. This could be the ticking of the clock or the beating of your heart. If random thoughts come in, just acknowledge them and let them go. The aim is to think as little as possible.

Centering

Centering is about ensuring that all your bodies—your physical, mental, emotional, and other subtle bodies—occupy the same space within you. Oftentimes, our physical body may be present in the room, but our mind wanders elsewhere and our emotions somewhere else still. Being uncentered weakens our energy field and makes us vulnerable to energetic and spiritual attack.

To center yourself, bring your attention to your heart chakra and visualize it as a magnet attracting the different layers of your aura to it. Take deep breaths while you do so, and notice how you instantly feel more present with and in control of your thoughts and emotions.

Grounding

Grounding ensures that you're energetically connected to the Earth. This is important for a few reasons.

First, the Earth is a powerful energy protector. When you're grounded, you benefit from its energetic stability and are more able to control your own energy, too. Second, being connected to the Earth during meditations gives you access to a constant stream of life-force energy that both cleanses and recalibrates your energy field. Finally, having an energetic connection to the Earth allows any excess energy that your body cannot handle to exit your being. This ensures that you don't get overwhelmed during meditation journeys, and that you're able to understand and interpret the information you receive.

To ground yourself, visualize an energetic cord extending from your root chakra and dig deep into the Earth. Visualize it pass through layers of soil, rock, and crystal caves; cross the threshold of the Earth's crust and into the magma; and tie itself around the Earth's core. As soon as you make a connection with the Earth's core, visualize any remaining tension or negative energy within you flow out of your being, through the cord, and into the Earth. Simultaneously, invite pure-positive life-force energy to rise up through the cord from the Earth and reenergize you.

CHAPTER 9

Hera

Goddess Hera, Zeus's wife and mother of the gods, doesn't have the best reputation, at least in mythology. She's usually portrayed as the jealous wife persecuting Zeus's love interests, namely Leto, Semele, and Alcmena; punishing Zeus's favorite illegitimate sons, Hercules and Dionysus; and casting her own son Hephaestus from Olympus because he was born crippled.

When I was growing up, my opinion of Hera was influenced by the extremely inaccurate but oh-so-entertaining TV series *Hercules: The Legendary Journeys* and *Xena: Warrior Princess* (of which I'm still a huge fan, despite the inaccuracies). Hera would rarely show up in person but instead appeared as two creepy, peacock-feathered eyes in the sky, accompanied by menacing background music. The perfect villain.

These mythological and pop culture representations contradict Hera's identity as the goddess of marriage, women, and family. How can the goddess who promotes marriage and protects women during childbirth also be the one who persecutes women and goes after Zeus's children? We're reminded, once again, that the myths we know are both slanted versions of the original stories and also allegorical. Surely there's a deeper explanation behind Hera's seeming wickedness.

I confirmed this when Sargis and I visited Heraion, Hera's ancient temple at Argos, Greece, on March 8, 2020. While walking through the ruins where once stood one of the most imposing temples to the goddess, I stumbled upon a marble block sculpted with two doves facing each other. Although not the goddess's sacred animal, doves are symbols of everlasting love due to their monogamous nature.

I felt there was something significant about this sacred symbol, so I sat next to it, closed my eyes, and sought to connect with Hera's energy in meditation. As soon as I tuned into her presence, I felt an ever-so-gentle wave of nurturing, motherly energy envelop my body. There was no bitterness, wickedness, or guile. Simply love.

Clairvoyantly, I saw Hera as a humble and protective mother guiding women and men to strengthen their parental instincts and awakening their desire for nurturing and family making. She communicated that she helps people create strong, loyal, supportive, and protective family groups, whether traditional family structures or other types of families, such as friend groups and other communities.

Interestingly, connecting with her energy during that meditation awakened within me a desire to create my own family (something I hadn't consciously desired previously), as well as to strengthen the bonds with my existing family members, friends, and online connections. However, the most important message she left me with was that even if we don't have a traditional family, we all belong to the human family. In the same way that plants, insects, animals, and all Earth-based beings belong to their respective species families, we're also in the human family, and that collective family is as important to nurture as any other one.

The Essence of Hera

Hera is the queen of the gods, as well as the goddess of women and marriage. Her name has multiple possible meanings, which are also mutually exclusive. According to Plato, her name stems from *erate*, meaning beloved, since Zeus married her for love. Plutarch, on the other hand, suggests that her name is connected to the anagram of *aer* (air), while another possibility links her name to *heros* (hero). Yet another explanation connects Hera to the Greek word *hora*, meaning season, interpreting the name as "ripe for marriage."

Hera is an earth goddess without being a representation of the Earth (that's Gaia and her daughter Rhea), and an air goddess without being a representation of the sky. Therefore, she's the intermediary between the earth and sky realms and gives life to everything inhabiting them. She's the air that gives life to all living beings, and the earthly experience of life in everything and everyone. When it comes to humans, she presides over domestic life on Earth, which is why she's the goddess of consummated marriage—the most sacred part of earthly life—and of birth and motherhood.

Hera is the Divine Feminine and Zeus the Divine Masculine, the two primal energies that make up the cosmos. Hera is the womb of creation, and Zeus the divine semen that impregnates it. Hera is the mother and Zeus the father of all creation. The *hieros gamos*, or sacred wedding, between Zeus and Hera represents the balance of masculine and feminine energy in all life, a balance that should be maintained for optimal well-being.

Although mythologically it often looks like Zeus tames or controls Hera, in spiritual truth she's not controlled by him, for without her divine womb no life can be born. Zeus depends on her as much as she depends on him. Consequently, Zeus and Hera were commonly venerated as a union that makes life possible, and an ideal partnership to look up to.

On a personal soul level, Zeus and Hera's sacred wedding represents the balance of masculine and feminine energy within us, driving our ascension journey. The golden Hesperides apples Gaia gifted to the couple stand for the infinite, cyclic nature of life and of the soul. Gold is symbolic of the indestructible and infinite, while apples are symbols of the soul. Thus, the myth can be interpreted as Gaia, Mother Earth, granting the sacred couple the responsibility of guiding souls through their multiple incarnations on their infinite journey of ascension.

The Triple Goddess

The Triple Goddess is a neopagan term coined by British poet Robert Graves in his book *The White Goddess*. According to Graves, many ancient goddesses from various cultures embodied the three phases of female life—the Maiden, Mother, and Crone. These three stages coincide with the three phases of the moon (new, full, and waning) as well as the three seasons (spring, summer, and autumn).

Although there's no evidence of the term *Triple Goddess* being used in ancient Greece, many Greek goddesses portrayed this triad of qualities, namely Artemis, Hecate, and Hera. The Three Fates (*Moirai*), Three Seasons (*Horai*), and Three Graces (*Charites*) were also triple goddesses whose characteristics and significance align with Graves's theory.

When it comes to Hera specifically, in Stymphalos, the ancient city of Arcadia, Greece, Hera was venerated as *Pais*, meaning girl; *Teleia*, meaning adult; and *Chere*, meaning widow, a characterization that essentially aligns with the Triple Goddess. Thus, this archetype provides a helpful tool for understanding and working with the goddess in a more practical way.

Not only can the epithets Girl, Adult, and Widow be literally linked to women's life cycle, as well as to the three phases of the moon and how these affect women's menstrual cycle, but Hera's three phases can also be applied to all people irrespective of gender, as well as all of creation. In fact, the three phases of the moon have long been associated with manifestation, a connection that dates back to ancient Greece, when the moon phases were deliberately used to optimize farming.

Let's dive into the three Hera phases and explore how we can utilize them in life and on our ascension journey:

- **Pais (Girl or Maiden):** Hera Pais is connected to spring and the new moon. The new moon energy represents potential and new beginnings. It's the first phase of creation, during which we plant seeds in the form of coming up with new ideas, setting intentions, and starting new projects in Hera's womb, so that she can nurture and bring them to life. In a literal sense, Hera Pais is connected to the purity and potential of early childhood, the first phase of a woman's menstrual cycle, and the sprouting of the Earth and her beings in springtime.

- **Teleia (Adult or Mother):** Hera Teleia is connected to summer and the full moon. The full moon energy represents progress, abundance, and completion. It's the second phase of creation, during which the seeds we've planted are now fully grown and flowering. It's the time during which our ideas, intentions, and projects have been manifested or developed, and we get to enjoy the fruits of our labor. In a literal sense, Hera Teleia is connected to the maturing and coming of age associated with adulthood, the second phase of a woman's menstrual cycle, and the fruitfulness and abundance of the Earth and her beings during the summer months.

- **Chere (Widow or Crone):** Hera Chere is connected to autumn and the waning phase of the moon. The waning moon represents releasing, reflecting, and going within. It's a time of change and transformation representing the third phase of creation, during which we let go of what no longer serves us, abandon goals and projects that have stagnated, and reenergize before we jump back to active creation. In a literal sense, Hera Chere is connected to the wisdom accumulated in our elderly years, the final phase of a woman's menstrual cycle, and the withering and recalibration of the Earth during the autumn and winter months.

Knowing how Hera's three phases or qualities relate to different areas of life, both literally and energetically, we can use the phases of the moon and the seasons in combination with Hera's energy to live life more fully. You'll learn specific practices for doing so in Part III.

Hera's Virtues

Hera's main virtues that you can embody to follow your purpose and path to spiritual ascension are fearless speech and pride or magnanimity.

Fearless Speech

The virtue of fearless speech, or *parrhesia* in Greek, is most accurately translated as frankness, or outspokenness. This virtue is about expressing oneself without fear or reservations, but instead with honesty, courage, and directness. It's about choosing truth over lies or silence, risking losing people and opportunities over playing it safe, being critical rather than bland, and choosing morality over indifference, passivity, or personal gain.

The reason fearless speech is a virtue is because speaking the truth often comes with risk and responsibility. Standing up to injustices and crimes takes courage, and unfortunately not many people have or are willing to develop it. How many times have you seen people be harassed or bullied in public and no one bothered to stand up for them? How about employers talking down to their staff while no one speaks up to defend them? What about the blatant experiences of racism we witness daily that we turn a blind eye to?

On many occasions in high school I was called homophobic names by classmates in front of the whole class, including the teacher, and nobody said anything. In London I witnessed a black female cleaner being harassed by an entitled white male in a public toilet, and none of the onlookers dared to say something about it.

Aside from these blatant examples, there are also numerous cases of microaggressions, such as eye-rolling, sarcasm, insults, and gaslighting, that we all witness daily and never speak up about.

There are many reasons why fearless speech has become such an underused virtue. The primary reason has to do with our current sociopolitical paradigm. In ancient times, people placed more emphasis on the collective well-being than on their personal well-being. People worked for the community and supported each other through life. Presently, we've undermined the importance of community living and prioritized our personal well-being. This has resulted in self-centeredness and social isolation, which limits our capacity for fearless speech.

Another explanation for our lack of fearless speech is the increasing influence of social media. Our social media addiction breeds comparison and uniformity, both of which prevent fearless speech. We've come to care so much about the way we portray ourselves online; the number of likes, comments, and followers we have; and how we compare with our peers that we're afraid to express our authentic truth for fear of losing followers or getting canceled.

When I first had the idea of launching my gay sex and relationships podcast *Can't Host*, I had huge concerns about how that would be received by my community. Having built a very niche personal brand online, I wasn't sure how my audience would receive this uncensored side of myself. In other words, I was holding back from fearlessly speaking my truth through the podcast for fear of distorting my online presence. I had allowed my online persona to limit my authenticity.

Fearless speech asks us to express our authentic selves irrespective of judgment or popular opinion, because it's the moral or ethical thing to do. On a practical level, fearless speech is very similar to assertive communication. It involves speaking the truth as a way of respecting emotions and needs, both your own and those of others. It's not about verbally attacking someone or responding in a passive aggressive way, but instead sharing your truth calmly, kindly, and unapologetically.

Pride or Magnanimity

Hera's virtue of pride or magnanimity, or *iperifania* and *megalopsuchia* in Greek, is best defined as the conscious awareness and acceptance of our inherent perfection and the excellence of our creations. Rather than vanity or arrogance, being proud of ourselves arises from being in alignment with the gods, and thus seeing ourselves for who we truly are. It's about seeing beyond our ego's self-perceived flaws and realizing the miracle that we are. Plato summarized it best when he defined magnanimity as the "magnificence of soul."[1]

Aristotle argues that "the man is thought to be proud who thinks himself of great things and is worthy of them; for he who does so beyond his deserts is a fool, but no virtuous man is foolish or silly."[2] Therefore, Aristotle makes a distinction between pride and vanity, arguing that pride is about recognizing and owning the things we're worthy of, while vanity is about feeling proud of things we're unworthy of or cannot accomplish. Connecting with Hera helps us find alignment with our inner being and instinctively know our strengths and worthiness.

Being proud of our gifts and who we are is also a way of honoring ourselves, others, and life in general. By recognizing our worthiness, we teach others how to see and treat us, and we also set an example for how they see and treat themselves. By being proud of ourselves we also recognize the pride in all of life, particularly the natural world. Minerals, plants, animals, and all of the natural world are unapologetically proud of their existence, something we can witness only when we're also proud of ourselves.

When we practice the virtue of pride, we open ourselves up to abundance. Since pride is alignment with our inherent gifts and authentic nature, it opens us up to knowing and following our life purpose and taking the action needed to fulfill it. When we show up for us by following our purpose, the Universe shows up for us, too, and we receive abundance of all forms, which allows us to live a more comfortable and fulfilling life.

Pride is also directly related to Hera's virtue of fearless speech: someone who's proud of themselves won't hold back their truth but instead will speak their mind fearlessly. Therefore, pride breeds confidence and self-respect, essential qualities to standing up for others and for ourselves when being attacked in any way.

Ascending with Hera

The practices in this section will help you align with Hera's qualities and embody her essence.

Activation Mantra

I am the womb of creation.

Taking a moment to center and ground yourself, place both hands on your heart or extend your arms up to the sky, and repeat this affirmation a few times or for as long as it takes to feel its essence. Rather than just saying the words, focus on embodying each word and truly understanding the meaning of what you're saying. Employ all your senses so that you can see, feel, hear, smell, and taste the qualities of the mantra.

Ascension Journal Prompts

Take out your journal and let yourself free-write your answers to these questions. These are meant to help you explore Hera's primary qualities in your life, creating opportunities for healing and growth:

- What has been your relationship with feminine energy?
- What parts of you need more nurturance?
- What's your soul ready to give birth to?
- How can you express yourself more fearlessly?
- What are you proud of about yourself?

Connecting with Hera Out in Nature

As the intermediary, life-giving energy between the Earth and sky realms, Hera can be witnessed in all expressions of life. She's especially present in couples, partnerships, and communities, and in all forms of families, whether human, animal, or natural.

Next time you're out and about, whether in nature or in a city, observe the groups of beings coming together in some kind of interaction. You may see couples holding hands, friends hanging out, family members taking a walk together, pigeons chasing each other, dogs playing, bees pollinating flowers, tree communities being formed, and more. Train your mind to look for communities of all sorts, and acknowledge that this is Hera's energy forming and strengthening these connections.

Take this a step further by thinking about the kind of energy that's being born out of these interactions in the form of thoughts, emotions, and experiences. In other words, how could the couple feel while holding hands, what's urging the pigeons to chase each other, what's the energy like between the dogs playing? The communities you witness can be thought of as Hera's energetic wombs, while the thoughts, emotions, and experiences produced are Hera's energetic offspring.

Orphic Hymn to Hera

Use this ancient Hera hymn whenever you need to deeply activate or call upon Hera's presence. Ideally, stand straight, extend your hands up to the sky, and recite the hymn out loud.[3]

> *You lodge yourself in dark hollows,*
> *and your form is airy,*
> *O Hera, blessed queen of all,*
> *consort of Zeus.*
> *The soft breezes you send to mortals*
> *nourish the soul,*
> *O mother of rains, mother of the winds,*
> *you give birth to all.*
> *Life does not exist without you,*
> *growth does not exist without you.*
> *You are in everything,*
> *even in the air we venerate,*
> *you are queen,*
> *and you are mistress.*
> *You toss and turn*
> *when the rushing wind tosses and turns.*
> *O blessed goddess, many-named queen of all,*
> *may you come with kindness*
> *on your joyous face.*

Hera's Symbolism

As you feel guided, use the following to invite Hera's essence into your home and sacred spaces. You can also use these symbols to set up a Hera altar, as explained in Chapter 23.

- **Colors:** Emerald green, light blue
- **Symbols:** Crown, scepter

- **Sacred animals:** Peacock, cuckoo, cow, hawk, goose, vulture
- **Sacred plants/fruits:** Pomegranate, lily, poppy, dittany
- **Offerings:** Lilies, peacock feathers, pomegranate, various fragrances of incense

Activation Meditation

Sit in a relaxed position, close your eyes, get into a meditative state using the Meditation Prep Process, then follow these steps to activate Hera's energy within you:

1. Bring your attention to your heart and focus on your heartbeat. Become aware of how each heartbeat sends a wave of life-force energy though your body, energizing and animating your whole being. Take a few deep breaths, observing this rhythm, and give gratitude to your heart for keeping you alive.

2. Let yourself become increasingly conscious of your physical body, as if you're discovering it for the first time. Starting from your toes and moving all the way up to the crown of your head, go through every part of your body and acknowledge its presence. This wakes up the consciousness within your body, allowing you to step into Hera's essence.

3. Call upon Hera's essence by affirming "I am Hera" mentally or aloud. Using the "I am" affirmation is a powerful mantra for embodying the goddess's energy. While repeating this affirmation, you'll eventually feel Hera's presence. You may see her with your mind's eye, feel her strength, or notice her through your other senses. Take a moment to acknowledge and welcome her.

   She stands there proudly, holding a golden scepter in one hand and a pomegranate in the other, and is accompanied by a glorious peacock. Her aura emanates a light blue light that instantly puts you at ease.

4. Placing her hand on your heart, Hera invites your inner Maiden to come forth, a representation of the Divine Feminine inner child within you. Your inner Maiden brings up the purity of your essence, the excitement of new beginnings, and the unequivocal trust in your capacity to live a fulfilling life. Let your inner Maiden energy expand through your body and awaken these qualities within you.

5. With Hera's guidance, your inner Maiden now grows up to be the Mother, the fully developed energy of the Divine Feminine. As your inner Mother steps forth, she instills in you a sense of confidence, maturity, and self-actualization. Let the Mother expand through your body and awaken these qualities within you.

6. Hera now invites your inner Mother to grow into the Crone, the final evolution of the Divine Feminine. This is the highest and purest version of your Divine Feminine energy, who brings with her the wisdom and knowledge she has accumulated through a life well lived. Your inner Crone shares with you the gift of releasing what no longer serves you and the wisdom to know when to let go and start afresh. Let your inner Crone energy expand through your body and awaken these qualities within you.

7. With the energies of the Maiden, Mother, and Crone fully activated within you, take a few more deep breaths in and let their energies merge and assimilate within you. Set the intention of embodying the Divine Feminine in all her forms and letting her guide you in living a full and fulfilling life.

8. Thanking Hera for this activation, gently wake up your body with small, slow movements and come out of the meditation, feeling great!

You can download an extended guided recording of this meditation at *www.GeorgeLizos.com/SOGM*.

CHAPTER 10

Poseidon

Before you start reading this chapter, search online for "Temple of Poseidon at Sounion" and check out the pictures. This temple had been on my bucket list ever since I saw these photos for the first time and read about its glorious history and importance during ancient times. Built on a cape at the southern foot of Greece, the temple provided not only a view of strategic sea lanes but also access to the three elements that Poseidon partly reigns over—water, earth, and air.

At this point in our temple-hopping trip, Sargis and I had been to at least five temples. During our visits, we'd lay offerings to honor the gods, meditate, and go on regression journeys. Following our meditation at the Temple of Poseidon at Sounion, we both noted that we'd gone deeper than in any of the meditations we'd done previously. We suspected the temple's location had something to do with it.

Here's an excerpt from the journal entry I wrote right after the meditation:

> *Earth shaker. I kept hearing this word during the meditation. In the same*
> *way that Poseidon shakes up the Earth with storms and earthquakes, he*
> *also shakes up our lives with change. He doesn't simply want us to embrace*
> *change, but consciously create it, too. Unless we create change, nothing*
> *changes. Growth and greatness are a function of our willingness to create*
> *and embrace change.*

At the beginning of the meditation, I felt the weight of my life's recent changes build up in my chest. I became overwhelmed with fear and anxiety. The uncertainty of what may or may not come or happen was unbearable. Right before my breaking point, I felt a door open within my heart and all the fear flooded out into the ocean facing me. Once my heart was emptied, I felt a deep sense of calm, security, and trust that whatever happens will be for my highest good.

Water, earth, and air. That's what did it! Their alchemy creates change but also the path to embracing it. The water's energy softened the walls of resistance around my heart. The earth below held me while releasing these emotions. The air created a steady stream that let things flow. In other words, Poseidon working his magic!

The Essence of Poseidon

Poseidon represents the element and power of water and all liquids. His realm of influence extends over the fluidity and unending flow and expansion of consciousness, whether physical or energetic. From a physical perspective, he's known as the god of the sea, rivers, lakes, storms, and all bodies and expressions of water.

Poseidon's sphere of influence also extends to the Earth. Water fertilizes the Earth to create transformation and new life. Thus, he was often honored together with Demeter, the goddess of the fertile earth. Poseidon is also the god of earthquakes and all seismic activity, and his name means "earth shaker." This also relates to the liquid element, as certain earthquakes can be caused by underground water currents, while most earthquakes are caused by the movement of magma deep inside the Earth.

From a spiritual and energetic perspective, Poseidon presides over the intermediary space that souls go to in-between incarnations. This space or dimension is etheric in nature and can be thought of as an ocean in which souls review and process their last lifetime and energetically transform before they're ready to incarnate again. Thus, Poseidon is one of the main gods guiding our ascension journey.

The myth of Poseidon's and Demeter's mating at Phigalia in ancient Arcadia is symbolic of Poseidon's spiritual dimension. According to the myth, stallion Poseidon pursued the mare Demeter to a cave below Apollo's temple where they mated and

Demeter gave birth to Despina (mistress). In this myth, the horse Poseidon symbolizes the mature soul about to reach enlightenment. The cave below Apollo's temple stands for earthly life and therefore the cycle of human incarnations we go through as we spiritually ascend. Apollo's presence is important here as he shines his divine light on the couple, a necessary quality for ascension.

Another facet of Poseidon's reign in the spirit world is evidenced by the Temple of Poseidon at Tainaron, who acted as an oracle of the dead. The temple is dedicated to Poseidon Asphaleios (Poseidon of Safety) and it was built in a cave believed to be one of the entrances to Hades's underworld. It functioned as a necromancy and oneiromancy oracle, where people communicated with the dead and explored the realm of dreams.

Poseidon's symbol is the trident, which brings together his physical and spiritual characteristics. The three spears of the trident represent the three elements that Poseidon claims some control over—water, earth, and air—and whose interaction shakes up the Earth, generates storms, shapes the coasts, and moves and cleanses the energy of the planet. We can also see the interaction of these elements in the spiritual realm, as Poseidon uses them to cleanse and transform souls in between lifetimes.

In essence, Poseidon is a god of change and transformation. He creates change through cleansing, shaking up, and transforming energy on both the Earth and in the spiritual realms. By keeping things moving, Poseidon trains us in embracing and better dealing with change when it comes up. He teaches us to accept change as a natural part of life and learn to ride its waves so we can evolve on our human and spiritual journeys. When we finally do so, we no longer see life's challenges as obstacles but instead as opportunities for growth.

Poseidon's Virtues

Poseidon's two main virtues that you can embody to follow your purpose and path to spiritual ascension are piety and goodness.

Piety

Poseidon's virtue of piety, or *eusebeia* in Greek, means to worship, venerate, and respect. Plato defined it as "justice concerning the gods; the ability to serve the gods voluntarily; the correct conception of the honor due to gods."[1] Thus, piety is about consciously, willingly, and consistently honoring and respecting the gods, others, and ourselves.

According to Pythagoras, to truly honor the gods we also need to honor their specific laws, functions, and institutions, including their political and social institutions. In his words, "If man would reverence the Oath, then must he do all in his power to understand the laws that govern this universe, and endeavor to preserve harmony and order in all things."[2] Piety is about thinking beyond our own personal well-being and working toward securing our collective well-being. Like the ancient Greeks, we need to shift from a "me mentality" to a "we mentality," think about the communities we inhabit (i.e., cities and countries) as living and breathing entities, and work toward creating well-being for everyone.

Since we're also part of the gods' essence, piety is about honoring and respecting others and ourselves, too. Socrates's student Xenophon shared that, according to Socrates, people's three most important duties are to be grateful to their parents, friendly with their siblings, and trusting toward their friends—all principles based on and extensions of piety.[3] In truth, piety toward the gods, others, or ourselves isn't mutually exclusive; to truly honor and respect any one of these, we need to honor and respect all of them.

As I shared earlier, while Christian propaganda has often stressed that the relationship the ancient Greeks had with the gods was transactional, that's far from the truth. Yes, many people had an impersonal, transactional, and often commercial relationship with the gods, but this is also the case with modern religions. The ones who truly understood the gods and the essence of the Greek religion sought to honor the gods for the purpose of embodying their essence and ascending on their journey, rather than to win their favor. Instead of following the dogma of religion, they saw religion as one of the many maps or pathways to ascension and used it mindfully toward that goal.

As the Stoics summarized it, piety is about living life as an unending ritual to the gods. When we realize that everyone and everything is part of the gods and the divine substance of the Universe, then every act we take on a daily basis has to be in alignment with the gods and their divine will.

Goodness

Poseidon's virtue of goodness, or *chrestotes* in Greek, was defined by Plato as "excellence of character."[4] Practicing this virtue starts with connecting with the purity of our souls and then expressing that in all aspects of our lives. Thus, practicing goodness is about being kind and loving toward others, being useful in society, developing and perfecting our skills and talents, and consciously striving for excellence in everything we do.

Socrates extends Plato's definition by stating that goodness is a necessary component for inner joy. When we consciously practice goodness in every area of our lives through daily action, we tune ourselves to the frequency of our souls and unleash the infinite well of joy that lives within us. For example, when we practice acts of kindness, dedicate time to our spiritual practice, deliberately work on improving our talents, and strive to be ethical and useful citizens in the world, we align with our inner joy because these acts are expressions of our true nature.

It goes without saying that goodness doesn't equal martyrdom or overextending ourselves. When we practice goodness, we do so because we've aligned ourselves to the infinite flow of joy that we have access to and direct that outward. We practice goodness because it's an expression of our alignment to the gods and our authentic nature, and we trust that life will return our kindness plentifully.

Ascending with Poseidon

The practices in this section will help you align with Poseidon's qualities and embody his essence.

Activation Mantra

I embrace change and transformation.

Taking a moment to center and ground yourself, place both hands on your heart or extend your arms up to the sky, and repeat this affirmation a few times or for as long as it takes to feel its essence. Rather than just saying the words, focus on embodying each word and truly understanding the meaning of what you're saying.

Employ all your senses so that you can see, feel, hear, smell, and taste the qualities of the mantra.

Ascension Journal Prompts

Take out your journal and let yourself free-write your answers to these questions. These are meant to help you explore Poseidon's primary qualities in your life, creating opportunities for healing and growth:

- What's your relationship with change like?
- What have you been wanting to do but are afraid to?
- How can you honor and respect the gods, others, and yourself more?
- What does excellence of character mean to you? How can you achieve that?
- How can you help create positive change in the world?

Connecting with Poseidon Out in Nature

Since Poseidon presides over all types of liquids, the easiest place you can encounter him out in nature is near bodies of water. Depending on what's closest to where you live, take yourself to the sea or a lake, river, or waterfall. Sit somewhere comfortably, relax your body, allow your eyes to soften, and stare into the water.

Mentally, seek to connect with the oversoul of water, and thus its spirit and collective frequency. To do so, think about how it would feel if you were part of that body of water. How would it feel if you were one with the ocean, lake, river, or waterfall, with all that it contains and its unique characteristics?

Then, take it a step further by visualizing your body turning into water and actually becoming your chosen body of water. Let yourself become the crushing waves on the beach, the stillness of the lake, the playful stream in a winding river, or the rushing gush of the waterfall. What can this body of water teach you about yourself? How does this body of water create change? How does this body of water deal with change?

Ponder these questions for as long as it feels good to. When you're done, visualize yourself materializing back into your physical body, and come back into waking consciousness by centering and grounding yourself.

Orphic Hymn to Poseidon

Use this ancient Poseidon hymn whenever you need to deeply activate or call upon Poseidon's presence. Ideally, stand straight, extend your hands up to the sky, and recite the hymn out loud.

> *Hearken, dark-maned Poseidon,*
> *holder of the earth,*
> *horse god, you hold*
> *the bronze trident in your hand,*
> *you dwell in the foundations*
> *of the full-bosomed sea.*
> *Shaker of the earth,*
> *deep-roaring ruler of the waters,*
> *the waves are your blossoms, O gracious one,*
> *as you urge horses and chariots on,*
> *rushing on the sea,*
> *splashing through the rippling brine.*
> *The unfathomable sea*
> *fell to your lot, the third portion.*
> *Waves and their wild dwellers please you,*
> *O spirit of the deep.*
> *May you save the foundations of the earth*
> *and ships moving at full tilt,*
> *bringing peace, health,*
> *and blameless prosperity.*

Poseidon's Symbolism

As you feel guided, use the following to invite Poseidon's essence into your home and sacred spaces. You can also use these symbols to set up a Poseidon altar, as explained in Chapter 23.

- **Color:** Cyan
- **Symbol:** Trident
- **Sacred animals:** Horse, bull, dolphin

- **Sacred plant/fruit:** Pine
- **Offerings:** Sea anemone, myrrh incense, horse-shaped tokens

Activation Meditation

Sit in a relaxed position, close your eyes, get into a meditative state using the Meditation Prep Process, and follow these steps to activate Poseidon's energy within you:

1. Visualize yourself sitting on an idyllic, white-sand beach. While breathing deeply, familiarize yourself with your surroundings by activating your five senses. Touch the sand to feel its texture, breathe in and let the salty air flare up your nose, feel the warmth of the sun on your face, attune to the rhythm of the crashing waves, and gaze into the endless blue facing you.

2. Once you feel settled, call upon Poseidon's essence by affirming "I am Poseidon" mentally or aloud. Using the "I am" affirmation is a powerful mantra for embodying the god's energy. While repeating this affirmation, you'll eventually feel Poseidon's presence. You may see him with your mind's eye, feel his strength, or notice him through your other senses. Take a moment to acknowledge and welcome him.

   He shows up as a tall, muscular god, holding his infamous trident, riding a chariot carried by dolphins, and surrounded by all sorts of water beings and spirits. His aura emanates a potent cyan blue color that asserts his authority across the ocean.

3. Poseidon invites you to hop on the chariot and join him on a journey to his crystal palace. As soon as you climb up the coral chariot, Poseidon prompts the dolphins with his reins and off you go. As you dive deeper and deeper into the ocean, you're joined by nereids, sirens, and other sea deities. As they surround you, they extend their hands toward you and bathe you in multicolored frequencies of light, cleansing your energy in preparation for your activation. By the time you reach Poseidon's palace, you've already released all stagnant or negative energy you previously had, and you're ready to receive Poseidon's activation.

4. The crystal palace is beyond anything you could ever imagine! It's made out of primarily white quartz crystals that help channel and amplify the ocean's multifaceted qualities. Looking around, you can see all sorts of fish, sea creatures, and water spirits, excited to see you and welcoming you to their home. Poseidon takes you by the hand and guides you inside his throne room, asking you to take a seat.

5. Extending his trident toward you, he strikes it on the ocean floor, turning it on and activating the frequency of change and transformation within it. The trident illuminates in a bright ocean-blue light that makes everything it touches come alive. Taking a step toward you, Poseidon hands you the trident. As soon as you touch it, the trident's frequency starts running through your body and energy, filling you with energetic vitamins that prepare you for creating, embracing, and dealing with life's changes. Take a few moments to allow the energy to saturate your being and charge you up.

6. When the trident's light has fully transmitted, hand the trident back to Poseidon and take a few more seconds to let your body settle. At the end of the process, Poseidon guides you back to his chariot and you ride together up to the surface. As you leave, the sea creatures and beings around you bid you farewell, inviting you to pay them a visit whenever you need their assistance or guidance. Stepping out of the water and onto the shore, give thanks to Poseidon for this activation and ask him to keep guiding you as you embrace life's changes and transitions.

7. Following the activation, gently wake up your body with small, slow movements. If you wish, take out your journal and use the journal prompts to channel more specific guidance, or make notes of the guidance you received during the meditation.

You can download an extended guided recording of this meditation at *www.GeorgeLizos.com/SOGM.*

CHAPTER 11

Athena

I'm writing this while sitting at the Acropolis Museum's café in Athens overlooking the Parthenon, which has been dedicated to the goddess Athena since the fifth century BC. I'm on a four-day solo trip to finish writing this book, but also to rest and enjoy what the city has to offer. After I wrap up this chapter, I'll hit the bustling Athenian streets and let myself wander in the city. I don't have a plan as to where I'll go, but I know it'll be an adventure. It always is. Athena always makes sure of it.

You probably know Athena as the goddess of wisdom and warfare, but as you'll learn later in the chapter, she's way more than this. Her unique set of skills makes Athena the goddess of civilization, which is why she was the patron goddess of Athens and many other ancient cities, and why she is closely linked to the magic and spirituality of cities.

When we think of spirituality, we often think of natural environments—idyllic beaches, awe-inspiring sunsets, magical gardens, and mystical forests. Yet, as much as I adore spending time out in nature, I also love practicing spirituality in the urban fabric of cities. Just like nature, cities have various flows of energy that, when utilized consciously, can lead to immense spiritual growth.

Specifically, each city has a unique vibrational frequency and personality that can activate deep wisdom within us. Each time I travel to a new city for longer than a few days, I return home a changed person. This is because when we leave our home city—to which our energy field is accustomed—and enter the energetic conglomerate of a new city, our energy field gets shaken, in a good way. The new city's energy introduces new qualities and variables that trigger repressed emotions, habits, traumas, and limiting beliefs, leading us on a new healing journey.

Athena is closely linked to this process. As the goddess of wisdom, warfare, and handicraft, she's guided the development of human civilizations for eons. Her wisdom, strategic qualities, and craftiness inspired humans to evolve out of the caves into villages, towns, cities, and the globalized world we now live in. Consequently, she's been responsible for the energetic molding of each city, providing exciting arenas for spiritual growth and the acquiring of new personal and collective wisdom.

The Essence of Athena

As I've mentioned, Athena is the goddess of wisdom, warfare, and handicraft, and the patron goddess of the city of Athens, from which she takes her name. As with many of the Olympian gods, Athena's birth story reveals the truth of her essence and the nature of her qualities.

According to Hesiod's *Theogony*, Athena is the daughter of Zeus and Metis, the goddess of cunning, wisdom, and good counsel, and is often described as "the wisest among gods and mortal men."[1] As the myth goes, Zeus married and impregnated Metis. However, when he learned that Metis was pregnant, he attempted to kill her, since, according to Gaia and Ouranos's prophecy, Metis would bear children wiser than their father. Cunning as she was, Metis transformed into a fly and tricked Zeus into swallowing her, then gave birth to Athena inside Zeus's head. Zeus experienced a severe headache and asked Hephaestus to split his head open with a double-headed axe—the *labrys*—freeing Athena, who came out fully grown and armed.

Zeus is the father of the gods, the divine intelligence and etheric framework that holds the cosmos together. Metis is the Oceanid goddess of wisdom who helped raise Zeus, strategized his plan to overthrow his father Cronus, and eventually became his consort. Athena is the combination of Zeus's and Metis's essence and shares both of their characteristics. The fact that she was born out of Zeus's head signifies her role as the Divine Mind of the Universe, and Metis's qualities allow her to use this divine, Universal wisdom for practical and creative purposes. Being born with the help of

Hephaestus, who carries the Universe's divine, creative fire, further demonstrates Athena's crafty nature and wisdom, which she fully and willingly shares with us. The fact that Athena was born fully grown and armed further shows that she brings her whole presence and wisdom, not holding anything back, to those who are ready to receive it.

Simultaneously, Athena's birth story also helps us understand the journey of the human soul and all other beings. Just as Athena was born and grew within Zeus's mind, we, too, develop our consciousness within Zeus's mind (the physical plane of existence) through our many incarnations. When we've learned our lessons and developed sufficiently, we evolve to higher consciousness planes such as the mental, spiritual, and Olympian planes of existence, portrayed by Athena's emergence from Zeus's head.

To the ancient Greeks, wisdom was not just mental and spiritual intelligence but also handicraft mastery. Hence, Athena's wisdom extends to the physical, mental, and spiritual realms. In the physical realm, Athena is the patron goddess of craftsmen, artisans, and all people who channel their wisdom in physical and creative ways. Whereas Hephaestus also specializes in handicraft creativity, he focuses more on the execution of handicrafting, while Athena is also involved with the overarching idea, framework, and plan needed to complete a project. We can also see Athenas and Hephaestus's relationship mythologically. According to the myth, Hephaestus tried to make love to Athena but she refused him, pushing him aside. When she did so, Hephaestus's semen fell down to the Earth and impregnated Gaia, who gave birth to Erichthonius, whom Athena adopted.

Athena's handicraft specialization also has to do with her overseeing the creation and manifestation of our desires, especially when they align with our life purpose. Whenever we create something, whether physical or immaterial, Athena is by our side, guiding the creative process. She tunes us into the wisdom of our soul to receive the guidance and mental and spiritual abilities we need to bring it to completion. Whereas Hephaestus provides the divine, creative fire and physical strength required by the creative process, Athena provides the mental and spiritual strength and wisdom.

Referring to Athena's wisdom, Plato shares that "when returning into herself... [the soul] passes into the other world, the region of purity, and eternity, and immortality, and unchangeableness, which are her kindred, and with them she ever lives, when she is by herself and is not let or hindered; then she ceases from her erring ways, and being in communion with the unchanging is unchanging. And this state of the soul is called wisdom . . ."[2] Therefore, we gain true wisdom when we align with the true essence of our souls. When we consciously connect with Athena through our spiritual practice, we find alignment with our soul and access the unlimited wisdom of the Universe we're part of.

Athena is also the goddess of fair warfare, self-discipline, and resilience, not in Ares's combative way but rather in the tactics, strategy, and discipline behind it. Just like in the case of Ares, warfare should be understood in a contextual, rather than literal, way. In today's context, warfare can be interpreted as interpersonal conflict and energy attack, rather than just actual war. Therefore, in times of conflict, Athena provides the strategic wisdom we need to come up with the best possible plan of action. Athena's warfare qualities are also associated with energy protection, and the goddess actively fights against all expressions of darkness, whether physical, energetic, or spiritual.

The way Athena was imagined in ancient times further highlights her protective, warlike qualities. She was often depicted armed with a shield and spear and wearing a crested helm and the *aigis*—a cape portraying the Gorgon Medusa. According to the myth, Medusa's glare would instantly petrify her victims; hence, Medusa's presence on the *aigis* symbolized Athena's ability to repel and diffuse incoming negative energy.

What unifies Athena's seemingly contrasting qualities of warfare and handicraft is the force of civilization. Through her discipline, tactical wisdom and creative force, Athena presides over the development of civilizations. According to myth, when the gods were quarrelling over Athens, Athena secured her place as the patron goddess over Poseidon by gifting the city the cultivated olive tree. Essentially, she provided people with the skills needed to utilize the olive trees' multiple uses—its wood, fruit, and oil. Similarly, Athena bridled the wild horse and built the chariot, made the ship to ride Poseidon's waves, and taught humans how to graze the sheep for wool.

Athena's Virtues

Athena's two main virtues that you can embody to follow your purpose and path to spiritual ascension are fortitude and quickness of mind.

Fortitude

Athena's virtue of fortitude, or *andreia* in Greek, is closely connected to Ares's virtues of courage and bravery. The main difference lies in the etymology and context through which *andreia* was used in ancient times. Etymologically, *andreia* is translated as "what properly belongs to men" and is best understood as manliness.[3] In late antiquity, *andreia* was used to connote endurance, martial courage, and persistance against death and other challenging circumstances during war. Thus, it was initially a contextual virtue tied to war and relaying the essential qualities of a hero.

Eventually, Plato and other philosophers extended the meaning of *andreia* beyond just the context of men and war to include women and other life circumstances. Contrary to the established tradition, Plato suggested that not only soldiers can manifest fortitude, but also those resisting fear and pain, fighting diseases, experiencing poverty, or facing a politically shaky situation. Later, Plato also applied fortitude to people who, as his teacher Socrates had said, "are mighty to contend against desires and pleasures," or people who exert self-control when faced with strong temptations.[4]

Specifically, Plato defined fortitude as "the state of the soul which is unmoved by fear ... self-restraint in the soul about what is fearful and terrible; boldness in obedience to wisdom; being intrepid in the face of death; the state which stands on guard over correct thinking in dangerous situations; force which counterbalances danger; force of fortitude in respect of virtue; calm in the soul about what correct thinking takes to be frightening or encouraging things."[5]

Essentially, Plato defines fortitude as a virtue of the soul rather than a manufactured sense of bravery in the face of life's challenges. When we align with our soul's higher perspective and wisdom, we can correctly evaluate danger and eliminate fear. We realize that no matter what's happening to our body or the physical world around us, our soul is untarnishable. This state of alignment affords us the knowledge that all is always well, and we're able to self-regulate in the face of life's challenges.

An important characteristic of fortitude, which is also true for courage and bravery, is that it's only a virtue when we practice it out of a genuine desire to create positive change, whether personal or collective. Therefore, fortitude isn't about facing fear and danger out of duty or for the purpose of showing off to others. Rather, it's a naturally occurring urge that comes from a state of alignment with our soul and authentic self.

Quickness of Mind

The Greek virtue of *anchinoia* is best translated as quickness of mind or mental agility. Plato defined this virtue as the "talent of the soul which enables its possessor to hit upon what is necessary in each case."[6] This virtue involves having the mental acuity to make fair value judgments and choices through careful comparison and consideration. It's about seeing things as they truly are and not being fooled by pretenses. Rather than being concerned with erudition or mental intelligence, quick-wittedness is more about having critical thinking and being street smart.

In a world in which we're constantly fed information, we need quick-wittedness to maintain our sovereignty. For the first time in the history of our planet, we have limitless access to information and ways of sharing it with the world. As a result, we're constantly bombarded with fake news and conflicting information that, if we don't monitor, can brainwash and disconnect us from our inner truth. Simultaneously, we've collectively become so skilled at camouflaging ourselves behind filters and virtual realities that it's hard to tell what's real and what's fake. When we align with Athena's virtue of quickness of mind, we're able to sift through the BS and only consume content and interact with people aligned with our authenticity.

Ascending with Athena

The practices in this section will help you align with Athena's qualities and embody her essence.

Activation Mantra

I turn knowledge into action.

Taking a moment to center and ground yourself, place both hands on your heart or extend your arms up to the sky, and repeat this affirmation a few times or for as long as it takes to feel its essence. Rather than just say the words, focus on embodying each word and truly understanding the meaning of what you're saying. Employ all your senses so that you can see, feel, hear, smell, and taste the qualities of the mantra.

Ascension Journal Prompts

Take out your journal and let yourself free-write your answers to these questions. These are meant to help you explore Athena's primary qualities in your life, creating opportunities for healing and growth:

- Think about the last city you traveled to. How did that trip change you?

- What's the wisest piece of advice you could give someone?

- What's your strategy for following your life purpose? Come up with a step-by-step action plan.

- How can you have more fortitude in the face of life's challenges?

- What practices help you have greater clarity of mind?

Connecting with Athena Out in Nature

As the goddess who merges craft and wisdom to build civilizations, Athena is best experienced in the urban environment of cities. My favorite way of connecting with Athena's energy is by going on psychogeographic walks out in the town. *Psychogeography* is the practice of exploring the connections between emotions, urban environments, and human behavior. It involves consciously disorienting yourself to disrupt habitual ways of experiencing spaces and gain new understandings.

I first learned about psychogeography during my undergraduate geography studies and then utilized it further while earning my master's in psychology. I now use it each time I travel to explore the city from a unique perspective, but also to witness and appreciate the influence of Athena in our lives.

Going on a psychogeographic walk is easy and fun. Firstly, you choose a *dérive*—an algorithm that you use to consciously disorient yourself in the city for the purpose of having a more authentic experience, one that isn't guided by obvious signposts. For example, you can superimpose a map of a different city on your current city and follow a random path, follow a specific color in the streets, or throw dice to choose which direction to go.

With the *dérive* guiding the way, explore the streets of the city in a mindful and inquisitive way. Don't just walk mindlessly. Activate your senses and take in everything around you. Admire the thought that went into the planning of the urban space, study the architecture and its symbolism, ponder the meaning of the art pieces you come across, and actively seek and appreciate hidden treasures that you may have previously missed. Most importantly, appreciate the wisdom and innovative craftmaking that went into the construction of the city—that's Athena's energy in its full glory.

Orphic Hymn to Athena

Use this ancient Athena hymn whenever you need to deeply activate or call upon Athena's presence. Ideally, stand straight, extend your hands up to the sky, and recite the hymn out loud.

Reverend Pallas,
great Zeus bore you by himself,
noble and blessed goddess,
brave in the din of war.
Renowned and cave-haunting,
spoken of and then ineffable,
your domain is
on wind-swept hilltops,
shaded mountains,
dells that charm your heart.
Arms please you, and you strike men's souls
with frenzy,
O vigorous maiden,
O horrid-tempered one,
slayer of Gorgo, O blessed mother of the arts,
you shun the bed of love,
you bring madness to the wicked,
you bring prudence to the virtuous, O impetuous one.
Male and female,
shrewd begetter of war,
she-dragon of the many shapes,
frenzy-loving, illustrious,
destroyer of the Phlegraian Giants,
driver of horses,
victorious Tritogeneia,
O goddess, you free us from suffering,
day and night,
ever into the small hours.
Hear my prayer and give me
a full measure of peace,

of riches, and of health,
accompanied by happy seasons,
O gray-eyed and inventive queen,
to whom many offer their prayers.

Athena's Symbolism

As you feel guided, use the following to invite Athena's essence into your home and sacred spaces. You can also use these symbols to set up an Athena altar, as explained in Chapter 23.

- **Colors:** Golden red, blue, gray, pale yellow
- **Symbols:** Aigis, shield, spear, Gorgon head
- **Sacred animal:** Owl
- **Sacred plant/fruit:** Olive tree
- **Offerings:** Olive oil, olive branch, myrrh incense

Activation Meditation

Sit in a relaxed position, close your eyes, get into a meditative state using the Meditation Prep Process, and follow these steps to activate Athena's energy within you:

1. You're in ancient Greece, standing at the entrance of the Parthenon at the Acropolis in Athens. You've journeyed for days to come here, to lay your offerings to the goddess and receive her blessing. The temple stands glorious at the top of the hill, emanating a striking golden-red light that declares Athena's power and presence in the city. You take a step forward and approach the altar at the entrance of the temple, lay your offerings, and open your arms toward the temple, inviting the light to cleanse and purify you before you can enter. Take a few deep breaths here and feel the frequency of the golden-red light wash through your energy, clearing impurities and preparing your energy to meet the goddess.

2. Once your energy feels cleansed, call upon Athena's essence by affirming "I am Athena" mentally or aloud. Using the "I am" affirmation is a powerful mantra for embodying the goddess's energy. While repeating this

affirmation, you'll eventually feel Athena's presence. You may see her with your mind's eye, feel her strength, or notice her through your other senses. Take a moment to acknowledge and welcome her.

She shows up at the entrance of the temple dressed in her long, draped *aigis* cape, fully armed with her Medusa shield, spear, and helm. The golden-red light surrounding her is even stronger and denser than that of the Parthenon, oozing protection and security.

3. Athena invites you to come join her inside the Parthenon and guides you to the center of the temple, where you find the imposing, 11.5 meter, chryselephantine sculpture of the goddess. As you stare up at the statue, you notice Athena's shield. Outside, it's decorated with an Amazonomachy and in the center the head of the Medusa. The Amazonomachy, "Amazon battle," symbolized the Greek ideal of civilization, while the Medusa was a protective amulet. Thus, the shield holds the essence of Athena's civilization-building and protective, warfare qualities.

4. The goddess now steps in front of you and places six energetic Medusa shields around you to protect every side of your body—in front of you, behind you, above you, below you, and to your right and left. She programs these energetic shields to stay in your aura for as long as you need them, both to infuse you with her qualities and also to protect you against all forms of attack. As the shields are planted within your energy field, take a few deep breaths in and let your energy field adjust to them.

    During this time, pay attention to incoming thoughts and impulses related to Athena's qualities, as well as specific strategies and action steps related to the manifestation of your purpose and other desires.

5. When the process feels complete, thank Athena for this energetic upgrade, walk out of the temple, and gently wake up your body with small, slow movements. If you wish, take out your journal and use the journal prompts to channel more specific guidance, or make notes of the guidance you received during the meditation.

You can download an extended guided recording of this meditation at *www.GeorgeLizos.com/SOGM.*

CHAPTER 12

Aphrodite

I grew up in Cyprus, the island where, according to Greek mythology, Aphrodite was born. My childhood was saturated with the art, stories, and myths surrounding the goddess of love. Everywhere you looked she was there, posing in her seductive nakedness in statues and paintings. School trips were dedicated to exploring her ancient temples and quarters, and myths such as the following prompted cheeky jokes among teenagers:

> *The genitalia themselves, freshly cut with flint, were thrown*
> *Clear of the mainland into the restless, white-capped sea,*
> *Where they floated a long time. A white foam from the god-flesh*
> *Collected around them, and in that foam a maiden developed*
> *And grew. Her first approach to land was near holy Cythera,*
> *And from there she floated on to the island of Cyprus.*
> *There she came ashore, an awesome, beautiful divinity.*[1]

I never truly understood the meaning and significance behind Hesiod's infamous story until my early twenties, when, disconnected from nature in my busy life in London, I was called to go back to my roots and reconnect to the Earth-based traditions of my culture.

Dissatisfied with my love life and drained of feminine energy, I flew back to Cyprus and drove to Aphrodite's Rock, the beach where, according to Hesiod's myth, the goddess was born of the sea foam and washed upon the shore. I had a single desire in mind: I wanted to know love more deeply, more fully.

Right then and there, I met Aphrodite, and love, for the first time.

As I walked into the calm, cool water of the Mediterranean Sea, I felt layers upon layers of sexual shame, limiting beliefs around love, and past hurts and resentments all wash off of my body. Hesiod's story finally made sense, love made sense, and I was reborn.

The Essence of Aphrodite

Aphrodite is known as the goddess of love, beauty, and sexuality. She's one of the oldest Greek goddesses, as she was imported to the Greek pantheon from Near Eastern traditions, such as the cult of Astarte in Phoenicia, Ishtar in Mesopotamia, and Inanna in Sumeria. In Cyprus, Aphrodite's birthplace according to the infamous Greek myth, she was venerated simply as the Great Goddess—a fertility goddess—long before the Greek pantheon came to be.

The two most popular myths concerning Aphrodite's birth are of particular significance, as they reveal Aphrodite's true essence. In the first myth, Kronos (the god of time) castrated his father Ouranos (Sky) and threw his genitals (or the Divine Masculine energy) into the sea (the Divine Feminine energy), where the divine semen along with the salty seawater gave birth to Aphrodite. Similarly, the second myth talks about Aphrodite being the daughter of Zeus and Dione, the former representing the Divine Masculine and the latter the Divine Feminine.

The symbolism behind both myths reveals the primordial nature of Aphrodite as the creative force of the Universe. Aphrodite is balanced in masculine and feminine energies and uses these forces to give birth to all of life. Her name comes from the Greek words *Aphros* (foam) and *Hodites* (wanderer), hence "foam wanderer." Her name further emphasizes her role as the life-giving energy of the Universe, which creates cohesion between seemingly opposing entities and maintains the perpetual flow of life.

Diving deeper into Aphrodite's symbolism, she was born by the swirling foam of the sea, stepped on land, and then rose to the heavens to meet her father, Ouranos (the sky). This union between the elements of water, earth, and air represents Aphrodite's overarching sphere of influence over all forms of life and creation. The mingling (*mixis*) of sea, land, and sky defines her as the ultimate creative force of the Universe, the cosmic creator that gives form to both animate and inanimate objects.

Aphrodite's essence is most potently captured by Monica S. Cyrino's definition of the goddess: "Aphrodite is sacred sex."[2]Aphrodite holds erotic power over all living beings in the world and represents the impulse toward intimate connection and union. As the sacred embodiment of *mixis*, you'll find her wherever the boundaries become blurred and new forms of life come into being. Hence, Aphrodite presides over and is the embodiment of the Law of Form. She's the Universal process that gives form to the cosmos and everything within it, which is why she's known as the goddess of love, sex, and beauty. In Cyprus, she was venerated as Aphrodite *Morfo*, meaning the one who gives form, in honor of her main quality.

The Four Aphrodites

Aphrodite's epithets in Greek hymns, myths, and culture reveal her various layers and qualities as they relate to her sway over the process of creation. What I love about Aphrodite is that she doesn't just represent the spiritual or romantic kind of love we're all familiar with from religious and spiritual texts. Instead, she embraces all forms and expressions of love, free from rigid boundaries and expectations. What you'll notice in the following qualities is that Aphrodite is equally a goddess of spiritual, sexual, persuasive, and self-love:

- *Urania* (**Celestial**): Aphrodite Urania is the embodiment and essence of Universal love, the core, life-force energy that both creates and maintains life in the cosmos and the Universe at large. She is present in everything and everyone, as she's both the active and binding ingredient in all of life.

  We often experience Aphrodite Urania in deep meditation, when our physicality softens and we melt into the oneness that connects us with everyone and everything. We also get glimpses of Aphrodite Urania in moments of spontaneous epiphany, spiritual enlightenment, and intense joy or love, when we align with the love we're made of.

  Aphrodite Urania represents the love that's most often described in religious or spiritual texts, and the state of alignment most people on a spiritual path aim to achieve. Embodying Aphrodite Urania helps us transcend the illusions and obstacles of the ego and physical reality, and understand that the basis of it all is pure love.

- **Pandemos (Popular or common to all the people):** In contrast to Aphrodite Urania, this is the side of Aphrodite that relates to the intimate contact and fusion of bodies for the creation of new experiences, whether for pleasure or new life. Aphrodite Pandemos is the sexual nature present in all forms of life, be it living beings or earthly processes. For example, ocean waves crashing on the beach, lava erupting in the atmosphere, bees pollinating flowers, birds entering their mating season, and people having sex for pleasure or procreation are all expressions of sexual love and the realm of Aphrodite Pandemos.

  When it comes to human sex, Aphrodite Pandemos is free from societal sexual or relationship stereotypes, rigid rules and structures, and expectations. She accepts and encourages all forms of consensual sexual expression without judgment or prejudice. Aphrodite Pandemos sees value in all sexual experiences because they all result in the creation of new life in the form of emotions, pleasure, and experiences, and thus, they expand sexual and Universal consciousness. As we engage in our own personal journey of sexual exploration, we not only actualize our inner being's desires but also push the envelope of what's possible for others, too. In other words, through our own sexual freedom, we contribute to collective sexual freedom.

  It's well known that the ancient Greeks were more sexually liberated than modern societies, as sex was also seen as a spiritual experience and a way to connect with the divine. In my home island of Cyprus, which was the center of Aphrodite's cult in ancient times, people honored the sexual and generating essence of Aphrodite by baking phallic-shaped bread during the Aphrodisia festival. According to Herodotus, Ennius, and Ovid, sacred or temple prostitution was also practiced in Cyprus: girls would offer themselves up for sex as a sacrifice to Aphrodite.[3]

- **Peitho (Persuasive):** When love is embodied, it has to express. Aphrodite Peitho is related to Aphrodite Pandemos and represents one of the processes by which we express love—through flirting, teasing, playfulness, seduction, and persuasion. These qualities are found in all expressions of life in various qualities. On a human level, Aphrodite Peitho drives our primal impulse for intimate contact and fusion with people. This force of persuasion is expressed in all our relationships—whether they are romantic, familial, or platonic—on different levels and depending on the nature and intimacy of each relationship.

We experience Aphrodite Peitho in our social dance when meeting new people, colleagues, and business partners; when making new friends; and when strengthening our bonds with family. We also express Aphrodite Peitho when we flirt, go out on dates, build romantic bonds with our partner/s, or engage in sexual activities. Simply put, any relational activity that requires persuasion, seduction, or wooing, in any degree or context, is the energy of Aphrodite Peitho.

- *Philommeides* (**Smile-loving**): Whereas the previous three layers of Aphrodite are concerned with either spiritual or physical love, Aphrodite Philommeides is all about self-love and exemplifies Aphrodite's popularity as the goddess of beauty (*kallos*) and adornment (*kosmesis*). *Kallos*, the inner side of self-love, has to do with the beauty we exude naturally when we recognize that we're physical expressions of love. When we connect with Aphrodite Philommeides, we realize that love isn't just within us; we're actually made out of love. When we align with this perspective, we automatically release all forms of self-doubt and self-judgment and witness both our inner and external beauty.

  Kosmesis, on the other hand, is the outer side of self-love and has to do with the process of augmenting our inner and outer beauty through self-care practices, but also with fine clothing, jewelry, fragrances, and cosmetics. Rather than using external adornments to create beauty, *kosmesis* works in tandem with *kallos*; we first appreciate our inner beauty and feel comfortable in our own skin, and then augment that with external adornments and practices.

There are many more layers to Aphrodite, but these are her four main qualities as they relate to human love and our journey of spiritual ascension. By embodying Aphrodite Urania, Pandemos, Peitho, and Philommeides, we embrace the vibration of love in all its main expressions—spiritual, physical, persuasive, and self-love.

Aphrodite's Virtues

Aphrodite's two main virtues that we can embody to align with her energy and support our spiritual ascension journey are friendship and generosity.

Friendship

The Greek word for this virtue is *philotita*, which literally translates to "friendship" in English. However, the full meaning of the word in Greek supersedes the way we define friendship today and encompasses various dimensions of love, with friendship as only one expression.

According to the ancient Greeks, friendship is a consensual spiritual connection between two or more people, founded on mutual respect, appreciation for one another, trust, dedication, and understanding.

This virtue was the basis of civic life in the ancient Greek world, which is evident in the importance the Greeks placed on hospitality. In Greek, hospitality is *philoxenia*, from the Greek words *philos* (friend) and *xenos* (stranger). Therefore, hospitality was about befriending strangers and treating them with the same respect that you'd show your friends. In fact, *philoxenia* was considered an ethical and religious responsibility—so much so that not being welcoming to strangers was a form of hubris and disrespect to the gods.

At its essence, the virtue of friendship is about treating everyone—friends, relatives, lovers, and strangers alike—with the same respect, appreciation, and understanding that you'd show yourself. The relationship we have with ourselves is crucial, as it's reflected in the relationships we have with everyone else.

From this perspective, to truly embody the virtue of friendship, we first have to be our own best friends. This goes beyond simple self-care practices and invites us to deeply love and accept ourselves exactly as we are, through self-introspection, vulnerability, and inner work. As a rule of thumb, you know you truly love and appreciate yourself when you're able to look into your eyes in the mirror, say, "I love you," and mean it without any hesitation or triggers coming up.

When we reach that level of self-love, we get to truly and fully know what the virtue of friendship is all about. Only then can we fully and authentically see and treat others with love and respect, as we recognize within them the same love we recognize within ourselves. As Aristotle puts it, being friends with someone is similar to two souls inhabiting the same body.[4] It's when both parties are so aligned with the love within them that they're able to energetically and telepathically coexist with one another in a state of mutual love, trust, understanding, and appreciation. Unfortunately, modern society often values individualism and self-sufficiency more than connection, community, and intimacy, which has distorted our understanding and experience of true friendship.

Furthermore, Pythagoras summarizes the spiritual and physical components of the virtue of friendship by dividing it into three categories: the friendship that the gods have with humans, that humans have with the gods, and that humans have with one another.[5] These three expressions of friendship beautifully emphasize how the essence of friendship and love is the basis of all that is, and the link connecting all life. It also demonstrates the process through which we can embody this virtue, which is through our conscious receiving of the gods' love, our deliberate extension of love toward the gods, and, once we've embodied that, our extension of it to other people, too.

It's important to mention that being friendly, welcoming, and loving toward everyone doesn't necessarily equate with being equally open and vulnerable with everyone. There are different expressions of friendship and love, and it's important to express love to others to the degree to which they are able to receive it. For example, we express love differently to our family, lovers, close friends, teachers, acquaintances, and strangers. Whereas we can express love more intimately and vulnerably with the people closest to us, loving acquaintances and strangers can simply mean respecting and living in harmony with them.

Moreover, loving everyone doesn't equate with not having boundaries or not protecting ourselves and our energy. Mutual love and friendship can exist only between people who are on similar vibrational frequencies and are similarly aligned with their authentic selves and worthiness of love. When people don't act lovingly toward us or immediately attack or try to hurt us, practicing the virtue of friendship is about taking measures to protect ourselves, setting up strong boundaries, and keeping our distance. Naively exposing ourselves to their attacks with the pretext of being loving isn't actually loving, because we're not being loving to our most important relationship—the one we have with ourselves. From this perspective, self-love or self-friendship takes priority and informs our expression of love and friendship toward others.

Generosity

Generosity, or *genneodoria* in Greek, is the virtue of sharing without the expectation of receiving something back. When we truly embody this virtue, we align with the infinite abundance of the Universe and share in the gods' inherent and constant generosity toward us and the cosmos. Generosity goes beyond acts of kindness; it is also a way of perceiving ourselves and the world. It's about disconnecting from scarcity consciousness and tuning into the inexhaustible wealth of the earth, the gods, and the Universe.

When we give to others out of true generosity, we don't really give away money, physical objects, time, energy, or the like. Instead, we extend the gods' authentic nature, and our own, toward someone else. True generosity is similar to the act of breathing. It happens cyclically, constantly, and instinctively. We receive the breath out of an inexhaustible well of air, and then we give it away to be recycled. We don't stress about the next breath being there or keep count of how many breaths we've given away. Instead, we've come to trust in the cyclic nature of our breath and trust that we'll be taken care of.

Generosity works in a similar way. We receive it constantly from the gods all day, every day, through the abundance of our beautiful planet. And, when we're tuned in to that abundance, we then give it away to those who need it, trusting that we'll receive it back tenfold.

When we're misaligned from this virtue, we experience greed, resentment, time or energy famine, or fear of spending or overspending. We buy into the ego's scarcity consciousness and stress over how much we get and how much we give out. This scarcity consciousness then informs our sense of self-worth, and we let our finances and material possessions determine how we perceive ourselves and others.

Being misaligned from this virtue also results in toxic generosity. This is when we give not because we genuinely want to help someone or because it's in our nature to do so, but because we want to show off, gain something, or benefit in some other ego-driven way. In the spiritual community, toxic generosity often manifests as spiritual egotism, where we give to others as a way of gaining favor with the gods or securing a seat in heaven. Conversely, true generosity comes out of an innate desire to help others, create social change, and benefit the world's highest good.

Ascending with Aphrodite

The practices in this section will help you align to Aphrodite's qualities and embody her essence.

Activation Mantra

I embrace all expressions of love.

Taking a moment to center and ground yourself, place both hands on your heart or extend your arms up to the sky, and repeat this affirmation a few times or for as long as it takes to feel its essence. Rather than just say the words, focus on embodying each word and truly understanding the meaning of what you're saying. Employ all your senses so that you can see, feel, hear, smell, and taste the qualities of the mantra.

Ascension Journal Prompts

Take out your journal and let yourself free-write your answers to these questions. These are meant to help you explore Aphrodite's primary qualities in your life, creating opportunities for healing and growth:

- What desires have you suppressed that are eager to be realized?
- Which of the four Aphrodite qualities have you neglected most?
- What limitations have you placed on your sexuality and sexual nature?
- What limiting beliefs prevent you from loving yourself more?
- What action steps can you take to practice true friendship and generosity?

Connecting with Aphrodite Out in Nature

As I've shared earlier, Aphrodite's love can take many forms: spiritual, physical, persuasive, and self-love. Depending on where you are on your human and spiritual journeys, you may currently need to focus on embracing one or two of these expressions of love.

Set the intention of discovering what expression of love you most need to focus on right now, and then head out into nature and let Aphrodite show you. While walking, look around and seek to identify various expressions of love. When you spot them, try to identify the kind of love that's expressed. Is it spiritual, physical, persuasive, or self-love? Or something else? Simultaneously, be aware of any signs and synchronicities that Aphrodite may send your way.

Once the direction becomes clear, take a moment to do a short meditation and try to nurture the emotion of that expression of love within you. Focus on your heart chakra and leverage the examples of the expressions of love you've identified to cultivate that energy within you, too. To achieve this, imagine energetic cords connecting your heart chakra with these examples, aligning you with their frequency.

Orphic Hymn to Aphrodite

Use this ancient Aphrodite hymn whenever you need to deeply activate or call upon Aphrodite's presence. Ideally, stand straight, extend your hands up to the sky, and recite the hymn out loud.

> Heavenly, smiling Aphrodite, praised in many hymns,
> sea-born, revered goddess of generation, you like the nightlong revel
> and you couple lovers at night, O scheming mother of Necessity.
> Everything comes from you; you have yoked the world,
> and you control all three realms. You give birth to all,
> to everything in heaven, upon the fruitful earth
> and in the depths of the sea, O venerable companion of Bacchos.
>
> You delight in festivities, O bridelike mother of the Erotes,
> O Persuasion whose joy is in the bed of love, secretive, giver of grace,
> visible and invisible, lovely-tressed daughter of a noble father,
> bridal feast companion of the gods, sceptered she-wolf,
> beloved and man-loving giver of birth and of life,
> with your maddening love-charms you yoke mortals
> and the many races of beasts to unbridled passion.
>
> Come, O goddess born in Cyprus, whether you are on Olympos,
> O queen, exulting in the beauty of your face,
> or you wander in Syria, country of fine frankincense,
> or, yet, driving your golden chariot in the plain,
> you lord it over Egypt's fertile river bed.
>
> Come, whether you ride your swan-drawn chariot over the sea's billows,
> joying in the creatures of the deep as they dance in circles,
> or you delight in the company of the dark-faced nymphs on land,
> (as, light-footed, they frisk over the sandy beaches).

Come, lady, even if you are in Cyprus that cherishes you,
where fair maidens and chaste nymphs throughout the year
sing of you, O blessed one, and of immortal, pure Adonis.
Come, O beautiful and comely goddess;
I summon you with holy words and pious soul.

Aphrodite's Symbolism

As you feel guided, use the following to invite Aphrodite's essence into your home and sacred spaces. You can also use these symbols to set up an Aphrodite altar, as explained in Chapter 23.

- **Colors:** Sky blue, green
- **Symbols:** Shell, mirror, knuckles (dice), sphere, her sacred belt (which could stop even Zeus's thunderbolts)
- **Sacred animals:** White dove, goose, sparrow, turtle, rabbit, white goat, swan
- **Sacred plants/fruits:** Rose, myrtle, pomegranate, apple, anemone (poppy)
- **Offerings:** Roses, myrtle, anemone, quince, apple, incense of perfumes and fragrances

Activation Meditation

Sit in a relaxed position, close your eyes, get into a meditative state using the Meditation Prep Process, and follow these steps to activate Aphrodite's energy within you:

1. Visualize yourself standing on the shore of an idyllic, white-sand beach, right where the waves crash upon the sand. (If you have access to the beach, you can do this meditation there.) Born in the water, Aphrodite stepped onto the land and then ascended to Olympus. Therefore, in this liminal space where the foaming water crashes on the beach you can feel Aphrodite's essence most potently. With your eyes closed, take deep, mindful breaths, and let yourself receive the crashing waves' energy.

2. As they crash on your feet, feel the waves' energy rise up through your legs and body, both cleansing and recalibrating your energy field. The waves

have been carrying this vital energy for hundreds, even thousands, of miles, and it's now released within your being.

3. When you feel cleansed and recalibrated, call upon Aphrodite's essence by affirming "I am Aphrodite" mentally or aloud. Using the "I am" affirmation is a powerful mantra for embodying the goddess's energy. While repeating this affirmation, you'll eventually feel Aphrodite's presence. You may see her presence with your mind's eye, feel her love, or notice her through your other senses. Take a moment to acknowledge and welcome her.

   She shows up completely naked, with only shells covering her genitals, and emanates a bright azure light. She is surrounded by a pod of dolphins, her son Eros, and the Three Graces.

4. Working via the energy of the crashing waves, Aphrodite starts directing the energy in a conscious way to activate her four qualities—Philommeides, Pandemos, Peitho, and Urania—within you.

5. The energy from the waves starts moving up toward your root chakra, activating the energy of Aphrodite Philommeides. Let your root chakra light up in a deep red color as Aphrodite activates your capacity for self-love and self-care. Breathe deeply while this activation is taking place, and let yourself receive this energetic upgrade.

6. As the energy from the crashing waves reaches your sacral chakra, it activates the sensual and sexual energy of Aphrodite Pandemos within you. Feel your sacral chakra lighting up bright orange as Aphrodite activates your sexual nature. Breathe deeply while this activation is taking place, and let yourself receive this energetic upgrade.

7. The waves' energy moves up to your solar plexus chakra now, activating Aphrodite Peitho within you. Let your solar plexus chakra vibrate a powerful, golden yellow color as Aphrodite activates the energy of seduction and persuasion within you. Breathe deeply while this activation is taking place, and let yourself receive this energetic upgrade.

8. As the energy makes its way into your heart chakra, it activates the energy of Aphrodite Urania, the essence of spiritual and divine love. Feel your

heart chakra's emerald-green light strengthen, as Aphrodite activates your awareness of oneness and Universal love. Breathe deeply while this activation is taking place, and let yourself receive this energetic upgrade.

9. With your root, sacral, solar plexus, and heart chakras activated with the four Aphrodite qualities, take long deep breaths, and let their energy move up and down through your entire chakra system and whole body, integrating and embodying these energies within you.

10. When the activation feels complete, express your gratitude to Aphrodite and ask her to stay with you and guide you toward expressing these qualities in their highest potential in your life. Gently wake up your body with small, slow movements and come out of the meditation, feeling great!

You can download an extended guided recording of this meditation at *www .GeorgeLizos.com/SOGM.*

CHAPTER 13

Apollo

On the sixth day of our temple-hopping trip, Sargis and I visited the Oracle of Delphi. I knew this would be the highlight of our trip, so we stayed there overnight and planned two days of spiritual activities to properly explore the site and connect with Apollo. And I was right! I had a powerful awakening experience at Delphi that changed my life and career for the better.

By that point Apollo had already been my favorite of the Greek gods. He was the god of divination, healing, and the creative arts, the three subjects I had been most passionate about my entire life. Apollo was my guy. I'd connect with him before giving a psychic reading, channel his light in healing sessions, and call upon his guidance when writing my books. In fact, I credited Apollo for helping me write my books *Lightworkers Gotta Work*, *Protect Your Light*, and this one, in the books' acknowledgments!

Consequently, I went to Delphi with high expectations, which were met to the fullest. The morning after our arrival, Sargis and I woke up super early to go cleanse ourselves at the Castalia Spring. The Castalia Spring is situated right next to the oracle and is named after the naiad nymph Castalia, who inhabits the spring. In antiquity, pilgrims went to the stream to quench their thirst after days of journeying to get there and to cleanse themselves before entering Apollo's sanctuary. The Pythia and priests of the temple also cleansed themselves at the spring before giving prophecies.

As I splashed the pure, cold water on my face, I felt it wash away fears and frustrations I hadn't known I'd been holding on to. An unfamiliar sense of calmness and purity came over me, grounding me to the present moment. Following the cleanse, we climbed the steep mountainside overlooking the oracle, getting as high up as we could to greet Apollo as he announced the new day, riding his sun chariot. We gazed in utter awe at the astonishing sunrise, as Apollo's sunlight slowly emerged from the Adriatic Sea over the verdant slopes of Mount Parnassus. I closed my eyes and let the light wash over me. Since I had cleansed myself earlier, my energy was clear and pure enough to receive its uplifting frequencies, giving me a spiritual high I have yet to emulate.

Our day proceeded with a long visit at the Archaeological Museum of Delphi, where we learned about the intricate history and glory of the oracle, and ended with our visit to the Temple of Apollo. Words cannot describe the emotions that coursed through my body as I walked up the path that thousands of people had walked before me to lay their offerings to the god and receive his wisdom. When I finally reached the temple, I placed my offering of wildflowers I'd collected in the morning at the main altar facing the temple and simply stood there, staring at its glory.

What transpired afterward was totally unplanned and unexpected. I'd somehow entered a semitrance state and felt myself guided to sit and meditate by the temple. Trusting the guidance, I sat right across from the *adyton* (the innermost area of the temple where the Pythia would go to receive Apollo's prophecies), closed my eyes, and went within. As I closed my physical eyes my inner eye turned right on, and I was surrounded by spirits of women that I intuitively recognized as the Pythias who served at the temple.

Help me deepen my intuition so I can help others do so, too. I stated my intention and waited. The exact steps of what transpired are quite blurry in my mind, but the Pythias along with Apollo worked on my third eye chakra and energetic field, performing some kind of psychic surgery to remove energetic obstacles and amplify my intuitive connection. Throughout the procedure, I tried to surrender as much as I could and let the process unfold naturally. Apart from the energetic clearing and upgrade I received, they also imparted practical tools, processes, and guidance, which I then used to develop my psychic abilities further.

But the most unexpected thing happened right before I came out of the meditation. While sitting there, I felt my hands wanting to move. Trusting the guidance, I brought my palms together and let them move freely. I noticed they were moving in a specific way, forming distinct mudras in a repetitive sequence. "Take my phone and film this," I told Sargis, who was meditating next to me. I was led to understand that this mudra sequence would help me continue awakening and amplifying my intuitive connection.

Following my trip at Delphi, I was guided to create and launch my online course *Intuition Mastery School®*. I used the tools, practices, and wisdom I'd learned at Delphi, as well as my 15-year experience as a psychic healer, to create a comprehensive, step-by-step program for intuitive development. In fact, I included the meditations, attunements, and original mudra sequence video from Delphi in the modules, giving students exclusive access to these sacred tools, too. You can learn more about the course at *www.IntuitionMasterySchool.com*.

The Essence of Apollo

Apollo has been described as the "most Greek of the gods," as no other Greek god represents so many of the ideals and standards of the ancient Greek world. A multi-faceted god, Apollo has been recognized as the god of truth and divination, healing and energy protection, music, dance and the creative arts, the sun and light, and spiritual enlightenment, among others. Mythologically, Apollo is the twin son of Zeus and Leto. His twin sister, Artemis, represents the Universe's purity and Apollo the Universe's light that enlivens the world.

Apollo was venerated at two major cult centers in the ancient world: his birth island of Delos and his oracular temple at Delphi. At Delos, Apollo was honored as a sun and enlightenment god; at Delphi, as a healing and divinatory god. Although the two cults focused on different aspects of the god, they also complemented each other.

Delos is a small but central island in the Cyclades, where, according to the myth, Zeus's mistress Leto fled to give birth to Apollo and Artemis after Hera banned her from giving birth on the mainland. At Delos, Apollo was honored as Apollo Delios, a name that, aside from its connection to the island, also means the one who brings everything into the light, makes things visible, and reveals the truth. God Helios was the personification of the physical sun, while Apollo represented the spiritual sun. Just as the sun shines upon and therefore sees and knows everything, so, too, does

Apollo know the truth about everything. This aspect of Apollo also explains why he's the god of prophecy and divination.

Apollo's (the sun's) spiritual light is also the life-force energy that all sentient beings need and utilize to grow spiritually, which is why Apollo is the creator of the Caduceus—the sacred symbol of enlightenment that he gifted to Hermes. Apollo's spiritual light drives the creative inspiration that flows through all life, as well as our personal and collective growth and development. Creativity, inspiration, and divine guidance are all expressions of Apollo's light as he guides us to follow our purpose and manifest our desires. It's Apollo's light that guides our soul's journey of ascension through our reincarnation cycle, and that contributes to the epiphanies, inventions, and creative ideas that have driven, and keep driving, the evolution of the human race.

Apollo is also the god that helps maintain the harmony of the cosmos. Just as the sun's rise and fall creates a stable, predictable, harmonious rhythm that keeps life going, Apollo sustains the rhythm and harmonious coexistence of the Universal laws. His association with harmony explains why he presides over music, but also over order, rules, and the law, known as *eunomia* in Greek.

The Oracle of Delphi, built on the rocky Mount Parnassus, was considered by the ancient Greeks to be the center of the world, which was marked by an egg-shaped stone monument known as the *omphalos*, "navel." At Delphi, Apollo's domains are healing, divination, and energy protection. Apollo's association with healing and medicine is connected to the healing and cleansing qualities of the sun's light and to Apollo's son Asclepius, the Greek god of medicine. The cult of Asclepius inspired the creation of the *Asclepieia*, healing temples considered by many scholars to be pre-cursors to hospitals. In fact, Asclepius's serpent-entwined staff, known as the Rod of Asclepius, is the modern-day symbol of medicine.

Given the cleansing qualities of the sun, Apollo was also known as Apollo *Katharsios* in Delphi, meaning Cleansing Apollo. Apollo's cleansing qualities are both physical and energetic; Apollo introduced the Greek world to energy clearing, purification, and catharsis. Today, the process of catharsis is best understood in terms of atonement or forgiveness, but for the ancient Greeks it also had a deeper meaning. Hubris was a kind of insult or affront to the gods, the city, or other people, similar but not identical to the Christian concept of sin.[1] To the Greeks, hubris created *miasma*—think of this as etheric staining, energetic mucus, or (as I say in my book

Protect Your Light) toxic energy attachment—which had to be cleansed for the hubris to be atoned.

Aside from cleansing *miasma*, Apollo's light can also be utilized to raise the vibration of people, objects, and spaces. Apollo's golden light has the highest vibrational frequency, and receiving it is the ultimate form of energy healing. That being said, receiving the full spectrum of Apollo's light requires perfectly cleared energy, purity of heart, and spiritual readiness. Thus, when we connect with Apollo, we can receive his light only to the degree to which we're ready.

The keys to fully receiving Apollo's light and wisdom were publicly inscribed on a column in the forecourt of Apollo's temple in Delphi for everyone to see. These three aphorisms, known as the Delphic maxims, were "Know thyself," "Nothing in excess," and "Surety brings ruin." The first maxim is the most significant for receiving Apollo's light, and it highlights the importance of self-awareness. It's a call to look within ourselves and see beyond the fears and limitations of our ego to reveal the true essence of our higher, eternal self. Essentially, this maxim invites us on a lifelong journey of doing the inner work. The more we do the work to peel back the false layers of the ego and align with our true essence, the more we're able to receive Apollo's light and wisdom along our journey.

As I mentioned earlier, the sun's ability to see and know everything explains Apollo's association with truth, prophecy, and divination. The central cult of Apollo's divinatory presence was at Delphi, during which the oracle known as the Pythia would enter a trance and receive messages from the god. As a result, Apollo helps us connect with our intuition and psychic abilities to receive clear guidance on following our life purpose and progressing on our ascension journey. I personally call upon Apollo before I do any kind of intuitive work, and in my *Intuition Mastery School* online course, I teach students to connect with Apollo as their main guide for giving clear and accurate intuitive readings and healing sessions.

Apollo's connection with divination and the workings of the Oracle of Delphi also elucidates the nature of fate according to the ancient Greeks. The Delphic prophecies are infamous, and often criticized, for being unclear and ambiguous, whereas in fact they were meant to be this way, and with good reason. Ancient Greek thought posits that we are, for the most part, the creators of our own reality. Yes, there are certain opportunities, obstacles, and circumstances we're fated to meet because we've agreed to them as part of our ascension journey, but what we do with them is dependent on our own free will and decision-making power.

As a result, the purpose of Apollo's prophecies at the Oracle of Delphi wasn't to impose actions, predict the future, or provide solutions, but rather to present the whole truth of the matter at hand, guiding people to use their own critical thinking to take action. Apollo making fortune-telling declarations and giving specific instructions would go against Universal laws and place humans at the mercy of the gods, which isn't representative of the ancient Greek religion. Greek philosopher Heraclitus explained the true aim of prophecies in these terms: "The lord whose is the oracle at Delphi neither utters nor hides his meaning, but show it by sign."[2]

Apollo's Virtues

Apollo's two main virtues that you can embody to follow your purpose and path to spiritual ascension are harmony and sincerity.

Harmony

The virtue of harmony, or *armonia* in Greek, can be defined as the pleasing combination of different parts to produce a common narrative. It's a commonly agreed assemblage, concord, or consensus that produces a harmonious result. Harmony is one of the most important Universal laws, as it coordinates all other laws to maintain the collaborative functioning and infinite development of the cosmos and everything it comprises.

For us, practicing the virtue of harmony is about living harmoniously with Universal laws, as well as with our commonly agreed national and global rules and regulations, for the purpose of coexisting peacefully on the planet. When it comes to the Universal laws, we can energetically harmonize ourselves to them by aligning with the frequency of Apollo's harmony though our daily spiritual practice. It goes without saying that our civic laws should theoretically be aligned with the Universal, natural laws, which unfortunately isn't always the case.

At first glance, when we observe the cosmos and its functioning, we identify a multitude of opposites and binaries that seem to contradict the law and virtue of harmony. In other words, how can the cosmos be in a state of harmony when we experience famine, war, and all sorts of destruction? Heraclitus believed that polarity is an essential and natural characteristic of harmony, both on a human and Universal level, saying, "Men do not know how what is at variance agrees with itself. It is an attunement of opposite tensions, like that of the bow and the lyre."[3] Therefore, the seemingly opposite poles of good and evil, creation and destruction, aren't really opposites but instead different expressions of Source—two sides of the same coin.

Heraclitus also explains, "God is day and night, winter and summer, war and peace, surfeit and hunger; but he takes various shapes."[4] All these states are expressions of Source and contribute to the harmony of the Universe. Each state exists on a unique vibrational scale that has two poles. Whenever we experience one state, we're automatically on its vibrational scale and have access to its high- or low-vibrational opposite. From this perspective, we can use this law consciously to transmute negative states into positive ones and move up the vibrational scale. Doing so is part of the creative process through which we develop on both a personal and a collective level. It's the process through which the Universe expands.

According to Pythagoras, practicing the virtue of harmony is about balancing our physical and spiritual natures.[5] It's about honoring both our ego and our soul so we can enjoy the pleasures of the world while not losing sight of our divinity. When it comes to harmonizing our physical body, harmony is about consciously bringing our body to a state of homeostasis. We achieve this by maintaining a balanced diet and lifestyle that respects our body and supports our physical health. It's also about balancing our emotional and cognitive functions so they communicate and work in unison to promote mental health.

Essentially, to achieve harmony of mind, body, and spirit, we need to deliberately balance and optimize each area, while also ensuring that we balance the time and energy we assign to them. Focusing solely on the mind or body will eventually lead to a soul-draining life led by the ego, while focusing solely on spirit will prevent us from enjoying the pleasures of life.

Sincerity

To practice Apollo's virtue of sincerity, or *eilikrinia* in Greek, one must share their truth clearly, honestly, and directly. Although this sounds simple in theory, it's easier said than done, as being truthful with others requires that we're truthful with ourselves. Unless we're willing and able to be truthful with ourselves about the state of things, then any truth we share with others will be tainted by our inauthenticity and self-denial. Simply said, it's not possible to be selectively sincere.

This is what the Delphic axiom of "Know thyself" means. To truly know ourselves, we have to be willing to see beyond the surface and unearth our shadow selves.
We have to consciously bring the shameful aspects of ourselves—our fears, traumas,
and limiting beliefs—to the surface and let them become part of our identities.
Unless we do that, the truth we share with ourselves and with the world is simply a
superficial persona rather than our authentic selves. Once we do this and *truly know*
ourselves, we don't need to try to be sincere but simply talk, feel, and be as we are.
Our alignment with the whole of us *is* the practice of sincerity.

The minor virtue of directness is closely related with the virtue of sincerity, and is
important to know and practice to embody sincerity. Directness is about expressing
our truth plainly, using simple words, and without trying to be diplomatic or manip-
ulative. Indirectness and diplomacy almost always have hidden intentions that smear
our words, thus obstructing truthful communication.

Ascending with Apollo

The practices in this section will help you align with Apollo's qualities and embody
his essence.

Activation Mantra

I am light.

Taking a moment to center and ground yourself, place both hands on your
heart or extend your arms up to the sky, and repeat this affirmation a few times or
for as long as it takes to feel its essence. Rather than just saying the words, focus on
embodying each word and truly understanding the meaning of what you're saying.
Employ all your senses so that you can see, feel, hear, smell, and taste the qualities
of the mantra.

Ascension Journal Prompts

Take out your journal and let yourself free-write your answers to these questions.
These are meant to help you explore Apollo's primary qualities in your life, creating
opportunities for healing and growth:

- What's true about yourself?

- What about yourself do you feel shameful about?
- What practices help you access your intuition?
- How can you bring balance and harmony in body, mind, and spirit?
- In what ways can you be more sincere with yourself and others?

Connecting with Apollo Out in Nature

Since Apollo is the spiritual presence of the sun, the easiest way to connect with him out in nature is by working with the physical sun's energy. As the sun makes its journey from dawn to dusk, it sends a wide range of vibrational frequencies to the planet. Think of these solar frequencies as energetic medicine or vitamins that you can consciously utilize to create change and transformation within your physical and energetic bodies.

The morning sunlight's frequency is full of the kickstarting energy we need to wake up and get started with our days. When we consciously bathe in this energy, we awaken our first two chakras—the base and sacral chakras—which boost our life-force energy and power up our physical body so we can complete the day's tasks.

At midday the sun's energy is at its peak. This intense sunlight frequency has cleansing properties, and we can consciously use it to clear negative energy attachments we may have caught thus far. It's also a highly energizing frequency that primarily powers up our solar plexus chakra, giving us the midday boost we need to complete the day.

In the evening, the sun's energy is much smoother. Its soft pink and purple hues activate upper-level chakras—the throat, third eye, and crown chakras—inviting us to wind down after a busy day. The evening sunlight frequencies also strengthen our intuitive abilities, amplify our imagination and creative visualization, shifting us from doing into being.

To receive Apollo's solar frequencies, get out to face the sun during all its three stages. Set your alarm early so you can meditate facing the morning sun, get out during your lunch break and let the midday sun cleanse you, and enjoy a gentle herbal infusion while gazing into the sunset at the end of the day. You can do this for a day or a week, or make it a daily habit for however long you need.

Orphic Hymn to Apollo

Use this ancient Apollo hymn whenever you need to deeply activate or call upon Apollo's presence. Ideally, stand straight, extend your hands up to the sky, and recite the hymn out loud.

Come, O blessed Paian, O slayer of Tityos,
O Phoibos, O Lykoreus,
giver of riches, illustrious dweller of Memphis,
O god to whom we cry "Ië,"
O Titan and Pythian god,
yours are
the golden lyre, the seeds, and the plows.
Grynean, Sminthian, slayer of Python,
Delphic diviner, wild, light-bringing,
lovable god you are, O glorious youth.
You shoot your arrows from afar,
you lead the Muses into dance, O
holy one, you are Bacchos,
Didymeus, Loxias, too,
lord of Delos, you are the eye that sees all,
you bring light to mortals,
your hair is golden,
your oracular utterance is clear.
Hear me with kindly heart
as I pray for people.
You gaze upon all
the ethereal vastness,
upon the rich earth you look
through the twilight.
In the quiet darkness
of a night lit with stars
you see earth's roots below,
you hold the bounds
of the whole world;

the beginning and the end to come are yours.
You make everything bloom
with your versatile lyre,
you harmonize the poles,
now reaching the highest pitch,
now the lowest,
now again with a Doric mode,
harmoniously balancing the poles,
you keep the living races distinct.
You have infused harmony
into the lot of all men,
giving them an equal measure
of winter and summer:
the lowest notes you strike in the winter,
the highest notes you make distinct in the summer,
your mode is Doric
for spring's lovely and blooming season.
This is why mortals call you
lord and Pan,
the two-horned god
who sends the whistling winds;
it is for this you have
the master seal of the entire cosmos.
O blessed one, hear the suppliant voice
of the initiates and save them.

Apollo's Symbolism

As you feel guided, use the following to invite Apollo's essence into your home and sacred spaces. You can also use these symbols to set up an Apollo altar, as explained in Chapter 23:

- **Color:** Gold
- **Symbols:** Lyre, bow and arrow, tripod

- **Sacred animals:** Wolf, eagle, swan, raven, crow, dolphin, ram, mouse, cicada
- **Sacred plants/fruits:** Laurel, sunflower, hyacinth, juniper, bayberry
- **Offerings:** Laurel, sunflowers, red roses, frankincense incense

Activation Meditation

Sit in a relaxed position, close your eyes, get into a meditative state using the Meditation Prep Process, and follow these steps to activate Apollo's energy within you:

1. Bring your attention to your solar plexus chakra, which you can visualize as a bright ball of golden light in the center of your body, right below your chest. Your solar plexus chakra is the sun of your body and being. It's the core of your essence and the place from which you can express your truth, through your intentions, willpower, and personality. Think of your solar plexus as the source of life-force energy that powers your body and your energy to express your soul's desires. With your mind's eye, visualize your solar plexus chakra turning on, in the same way you'd turn on the light in a dark room. As it turns on, breathe deeply and visualize its light growing bigger with each breath.

2. Once your solar plexus chakra is turned on, call upon Apollo's essence by affirming "I am Apollo" mentally or aloud. Using the "I am" affirmation is a powerful mantra for embodying the god's energy. While repeating this affirmation, you'll eventually feel Apollo's presence. You may see him with your mind's eye, feel his strength, or notice him through your other senses. Take a moment to acknowledge and welcome him.

   He shows up as a young, handsome, beardless man with long hair, wearing a crown of laurel leaves and playing his golden lyre. His aura radiates a glorious golden light—the sun's spiritual light—that connects with the energy of your solar plexus chakra, lighting it up even more.

3. Before you can fully receive his light and wisdom, Apollo first needs to cleanse your energy field. Placing his fingers on the lyre's strings, he starts playing the most beautiful musical harmonies you've ever heard. These are cleansing and purifying frequencies that work on the subtle layers of your being to cleanse your chakras and aura. Stay still and breathe deeply during

this process and let the frequencies saturate your whole being, releasing any energetic attachments that are clogging your field.

4. With your energy field fully cleansed, you're ready to receive Apollo's golden light to the degree to which you're spiritually ready. Apollo extends his hand toward you and starts beaming the Golden Ray of Source to your solar plexus chakra. The Golden Ray is spiritual solar light. It has the highest frequency there can be, as it is the frequency of the Universe. When you align with the Golden Ray, you access the truth of your soul and the collective wisdom of the Universe. From this state of alignment, you no longer ask questions, you simply know the answers. You don't second-guess yourself or your purpose. You know exactly who you are and what you're here to do.

    As the Golden Ray fills up your solar plexus chakra, let the light expand to the other six chakras, your body, and your aura so you're enveloped in a cocoon of golden light. Stay in this state for a while, letting yourself melt into the energy.

5. While you're surrounded by the Golden Ray, spend some time thinking about who you are, what your purpose is, as well as the current stage on your life's and soul's journeys. Ask any questions you have about yourself and about life, and let yourself receive the answers. You may do so via thoughts, feelings, sounds, visions, or simply a deep sense of knowing.

6. When the process feels complete, bring both of your hands to your chest and visualize your chest as a magnet, drawing the golden energy inside your body. Let yourself absorb this energy so you can embody the wisdom you receive and easily access it along your journey.

7. Thank Apollo for this energetic upgrade and gently wake up your body with small, slow movements. If you wish, take out your journal and use the journal prompts to channel more specific guidance, or make notes of the guidance you received during the meditation.

You can download an extended guided recording of this meditation at www.GeorgeLizos.com/SOGM.

CHAPTER 14

Hermes

I got a 52 on my first high school English test. I was a 12-year-old perfectionist who only got straight As, so my barely passing grade was unacceptable. I was devastated. I'd just transferred to a private English high school in Cyprus, wanting to make a fresh start. The only problem was, I didn't speak the language. Yes, I knew enough to communicate, but that only got me a 52.

As the years went by, I worked my ass off to improve my English, graduated top of my class, and got into one of the top universities in the UK. My English eventually became better than my Greek, to the point that I had trouble expressing myself in Greek! Yet, that first English test had scarred me. I was 22 at the time and I'd just started writing my first book, *Be the Guru*. I was confident about the message I wanted to share and the practices I wanted to include, yet my inner critic was pummeling me with judgment:

> *Who are you to write a book?*
> *English isn't even your first language.*
> *You don't communicate clearly.*
> *You're not a good writer.*
> *You can't do this.*
> *Give up.*

I kept writing and rewriting the book. I'd graduated college, went on to do a master's degree, got my first job in London, and I was still writing that freaking book! It still hadn't felt good enough to publish. Better said, *I* hadn't felt good enough to publish it. Until one day I decided that enough was enough. The book had to get published. But to do that, I had to get over my insecurities and show my perfectionism the door.

Right about that time I'd started reading about Greek spirituality and the gods and goddesses. I'd always felt an affinity with Hermes. From what I remembered in mythology, he was a messenger god who helped with communication and language. So I decided to ask him for help. I set up an altar in my room with a statue of him that I bought in Athens the year before, adorned it with his symbols and other offerings I'd read about in books, lit a candle, closed my eyes, and talked to him: *Help me find the confidence to publish this book. Help me know my worth.*

No, my fears and limiting beliefs didn't instantly vanish. It took a while. And no, the spirit of Hermes didn't materialize in front of me to deliver a prophecy. But as soon as I set up the altar and opened myself up for help, something shifted within me. In the weeks and months that followed, I was guided on a journey that helped me soften my perfectionism, release my limiting beliefs, and boost my self-confidence.

Rather than the grand spiritual epiphany that we usually expect when communicating with deities, the god had worked through other communication means to help me. He led me to books, people, and workshops. He orchestrated meetings and synchronicities. He helped me shift my thoughts, process my emotions, and safely access and heal my traumas. A year later, *Be the Guru* was written and published.

That's when Hermes's role as a messenger truly made sense. Hermes is the conversations we have, the people we meet, the books we read, and all the ways through which we receive guidance and messages from the Universe. He's the function of communication itself—the idea that once you tune in, you can receive the answers to any and all questions you may possibly have.

The Essence of Hermes

Hermes is commonly known as the messenger of the gods, and this is true on many levels. On a human level, he's the god presiding over our cognitive functions and all forms of communication, such as language, writing, commerce, diplomacy, and persuasion. Hence, he's a protector and guide for authors, speakers, entrepreneurs, and anyone requiring clear communication to do their work. Hermes is also the god closest to humans and dedicated to helping us find our way, follow our purpose, and live fulfilling lives. This is why he's the foreman and caretaker of roads, whether physical or metaphorical.

In fact, the name *Hermes* is derived from the Greek *herma*, which means "stone heap" and is most commonly known as a *herm*. Herms were square, stone pillars with a sculpted head, sometimes a torso, and genitals carved at the appropriate height. They usually featured Hermes and were placed at various boundaries, such as outside of houses, in front of temples and other public buildings, and at crossings and borders. The herms had a protective and apotropaic function; they were used to ward off negative energy and bring in luck, safety, stability, and protection.

On a spiritual level, Hermes guides souls on their journey of spiritual ascension. His creation myth is a symbolic representation of this journey. According to the myth, Hermes was born in a cave in Cylene, Arcadia. The cave symbolizes physical matter and the cycle of incarnations that a human soul has to go through until they ascend to the higher planes of existence. Four hours after his birth, Hermes received a turtle shell—a stable structure symbolizing immortality and the perfected soul. He put seven chords on the turtle shell to create a lyre, representing the seven spiritual centers, or chakras, that all humans need to evolve spiritually. Thus, the lyre is a divine instrument that helps harmonize the seven chakras and guide our journey of ascension. Additionally, the symbolism of the number 4 has to do with the four communication gifts Hermes gave to humanity: speech (*logos*), the art of fighting, the musical scale, and geometry.

On his first day alive, Hermes stole 50 cows from Apollo and sacrificed two of them to the other gods. Apollo's cows symbolize the divine, solar, life-force energy that we need to activate our seven spiritual centers and advance on our ascension journey. Apollo then gifted Hermes the Caduceus, a rod symbolizing spiritual perfection and enlightenment. The Caduceus is golden, signifying the end of the cycle of human incarnations and the transition to the higher planes of existence, and it's surrounded by two snakes intertwined at four points, symbolizing the pacification of the opposites as well as the four elements of earth, air, fire, and water.

Hermes's sacrifice of the two cows to the other gods also communicates the importance of working with all 12 gods on the ascension journey. This further establishes him as a communication god, acting as a bridge between the physical and spiritual planes of existence.

To complete the ascension journey, Hermes needed the wisdom and qualities of all 12 gods; thus, according to the myth, he stole the gods' symbols. For example, in the *Odyssey*, he stole Poseidon's trident, Artemis's arrows, and Aphrodite's belt.

From this perspective, Hermes is also a *psychopompos*, or psychopomp, literally meaning "the guide of souls." He accompanies human souls during their deaths, guiding their path forward. Consequently, we can sum up Hermes as the great protector of the human soul, guiding our souls' journey on the planet and through our many incarnations, until we've reached spiritual enlightenment.

In Archaic Greece, Hermes was usually portrayed as a bearded, mature man who was dressed as a herald, traveler, or shepherd, while in Classical and Hellenistic Greece, he was largely represented as a young, athletic man without a beard. Hermes was portrayed with various symbolic objects: the *petasos*, a white-brimmed hat that was sometimes adorned with a pair of small wings; the Caduceus; and *pedila*, sandals that were also sometimes depicted with wings and symbolized his aptitude in communication.

Hermes's Virtues

Hermes's two main virtues that you can embody to follow your purpose and path to spiritual ascension are fair dealing and sociability.

Fair Dealing

The virtue of fair dealing, or *eusunallaxia* in Greek, is a subvirtue of Zeus's virtue of justice, and it has to do with acting in a just and honest way in our dealings and interactions. It's about doing what's good and right for everyone, and providing services and splitting goods fairly. This virtue also presupposes that all parties partake in dealings willingly, and there's no form of blackmailing or manipulation.

On first look, this virtue may seem to oppose Hermes's reputation as the "divine trickster" and the patron god of thieves. In fact, his epithet *Dolios*, "tricky," refers to his proclivities for cheating, scheming, and deceiving, which contradict the virtue of fair dealing. However, as we've seen and discussed, myths aren't meant to be taken literally but should instead be interpreted philosophically to obtain their real meaning. In the case of Hermes, we've seen how his stealing of the gods' symbols and possessions is a metaphor for the qualities we need to progress on our ascension journey, rather than an encouragement to commit crime.

Sociability

The virtue of sociability, or *eukoinonesia* in Greek, is about the importance of embracing our social nature and human connection in living a fulfilling life and evolving spiritually. When we align with this virtue, we engage and socialize with other people with ease and are actively involved in society. In fact, communication, one of Hermes's main qualities, stems from the word *community* (this is also true in Greek). This explains the deeper meaning of communication as the process of being active and deliberate participants in society.

Modern, founded religions, such as Christianity, often diminish the importance of sociability in spiritual growth. Instead, they encourage asceticism and place greater emphasis on a personal—therefore, lonely—journey of saving one's soul. Although such religions encourage deep connection with God, they overlook the power of spiritual growth through community. Simultaneously, modern society in general is molded that way, too; despite our increasing global connectedness, we live incredibly isolated lives that lack community, and therefore, communication.

Ascending with Hermes

The practices in this section will help you align with Hermes's qualities and embody his essence.

Activation Mantra

I am guided at all times.

Taking a moment to center and ground yourself, place both hands on your heart or extend your arms up to the sky, and repeat this affirmation a few times or for as long as it takes to feel its essence. Rather than just saying the words, focus on embodying each word and truly understanding the meaning of what you're saying. Employ all your senses so that you can see, feel, hear, smell, and taste the qualities of the mantra.

Ascension Journal Prompts

Take out your journal and let yourself free-write your answers to these questions. These are meant to help you explore Hermes's primary qualities in your life, creating opportunities for healing and growth:

- If you only had one more day on this planet, what would you communicate and to whom?
- What's blocking you from expressing yourself clearly and authentically?
- What skills do you need to develop to follow your purpose more fully?
- How can you be fairer in your interactions with people?
- How have your friendships and relationships contributed to your spiritual growth?

Connecting with Hermes Out in Nature

As the god of crossroads and communication, Hermes is constantly sending us messages to help guide our life purpose and ascension journey. As I mentioned earlier, Hermes's messages can come through all kinds of sources: people, books, signs, synchronicities, and nature.

A great way to actively communicate with and receive messages from Hermes is to ask him a specific question and get out in nature to receive the answer. You may want to seek guidance on the next steps for following your purpose, have a problem you'd like a solution to, or want a specific question answered. Whatever it is, frame your question in a specific way and then go for a walk out in nature with the intention of receiving the answers and guidance you need.

Before you head out, it's a good idea to go through the Meditation Prep Process so that you're centered, grounded, and ready to receive guidance. Once you're out, the guidance you seek can come from everything and everyone. It may be in the butterfly that's just flown by your face, the synchronized movement of the birds in the sky, or the heart-shaped pebble you happen to spot on the beach. One summer, I was in the sea chatting with a friend about a challenge she was facing, when a school of little fish started leaping over the surface of the water around us. We were both in awe and knew this was divine communication.

As a rule of thumb, messages from spirit come in unusual and spontaneous ways, so keep an eye out for such occurrences. Once you receive the sign/s, your ego will most probably come in to doubt it, so be mindful of that and don't let it sabotage the process. Be sure to have your journal with you and take notes of any additional intuitive guidance that comes in as a result. You can read more about asking for and recognizing signs from the gods in the appendices.

Orphic Hymn to Hermes

Use this ancient Hermes hymn whenever you need to deeply activate or call upon Hermes's presence. Ideally, stand straight, extend your hands up to the sky, and recite the hymn out loud.

> Hear me, Hermes,
> messenger of Zeus, son of Maia,
> almighty in heart, lord of the deceased,
> judge of contests,
> gentle and clever, O Argeiphontes,
> you are the guide
> of the flying sandals,
> a man-loving prophet to mortals.
> A vigorous god, you delight
> in exercise and in deceit.
> Interpreter of all you are
> and a profiteer who frees us of cares,
> who holds in his hands
> the blameless tool of peace.
> Lord of Korykos, blessed,
> helpful, and skilled in words,
> you assist in work and you are
> a friend of mortals in need.
> You wield the dreaded, the respected
> weapon of speech.
> Hear my prayer and grant
> a good end to a life of industry,
> gracious talk,
> and mindfulness.

Hermes's Symbolism

As you feel guided, use the following to invite Hermes's essence into your home and sacred spaces. You can also use these symbols to set up a Hermes altar, as explained in Chapter 23.

- **Colors:** Silver, saffron, gold
- **Symbols:** Winged sandals, phallus, Caduceus, shepherd's flute
- **Sacred animals:** Dog, seagull, cock, cow, ram, hawk, turtle, hare
- **Sacred plants/fruits:** Wild strawberry, saffron frankincense and styrax incense, mint for Hermes Cthonios
- **Offerings:** Tongue-shaped tokens, rosemary, almond tree, pine tree, frankincense incense

Activation Meditation

Sit in a relaxed position, close your eyes, get into a meditative state using the Meditation Prep Process, and follow these steps to activate Hermes's energy within you:

1. Bring your attention to your heart chakra in the center of your chest. Just as your physical heart keeps your body alive and vital, your spiritual heart regulates your connection with your spiritual nature and higher planes of existence. Think of it as the doorway to your soul. As the midpoint of your seven chakras, the heart chakra is also the bridge between your lower, physical chakras, and your upper, spiritual chakras. Therefore, your heart chakra facilitates the communication between your physical and spiritual natures. Take a few deep breaths in while concentrating on your physical heart and heart chakra, and acknowledge all the ways they take care of your body and being.

2. Call upon Hermes's essence by affirming "I am Hermes" mentally or aloud. Using the "I am" affirmation is a powerful mantra for embodying the god's energy. While repeating this affirmation, you'll eventually feel Hermes's presence. You may see him with your mind's eye, feel his strength, or notice him through your other senses. Take a moment to acknowledge and welcome him.

He shows up hovering slightly above the ground and possibly flying around you with his winged hat and sandals, holding the Caduceus in his hands and emanating a magnificent silver light.

3. As he approaches you, Hermes extends the Caduceus right in front of your heart to perform an activation. As mentioned previously, the Caduceus is an instrument of spiritual perfection and enlightenment. It holds the frequency of the perfected soul, and thus can speed up the journey of ascension. Gently touching your heart chakra with the tip of the Caduceus, Hermes activates all seven auric layers of your heart chakra and opens the doorway to your soul.

4. Breathe deeply several times and let the golden light that now emanates from your heart expand outward and saturate your entire physical body and auric field. This golden light is the frequency of your soul. As it seeps through your body and aura, it awakens all parts of you to their highest frequency and potential, reminding them that you're an eternal, spiritual being having a human experience. It dissolves the hold of the ego over you, allowing you to see your life, other people, and the world from a higher perspective.

5. Following the activation of your heart chakra, Hermes proceeds by touching your feet with the Caduceus and adorning them with a pair of golden, etheric winged sandals. As they flutter their wings, they activate your capacity to speed up your soul's ascension journey as well as your current life's journey to follow and fulfill your purpose. Take a few deep breaths in and feel the shift in your energy as a result of Hermes's gift.

6. Before you come out of the meditation, take a few moments to register how your energy has shifted as a result of both activations. Set the intention of maintaining this alignment and higher perspective, and let yourself imagine the evolution of your life's and soul's journey. In this state of alignment, you're also able to receive clearer guidance from Hermes and your other spirit guides. Let yourself receive that.

7. When the process feels complete, thank Hermes for this activation and gently wake up your body with small, slow movements. If you wish, take out

your journal and use the journal prompts to channel more specific guidance, or make notes of the guidance you received during the meditation.

You can download an extended guided recording of this meditation at *www.GeorgeLizos.com/SOGM.*

CHAPTER 15

Zeus

The final stop on our temple-hopping trip was the Temple of Zeus in Olympia, the birthplace of the Olympic Games and the center of the cult of Zeus in the ancient world. After a long road trip, we reached Olympia in the evening and checked in to our hotel, only to find out from the hotel owner that the government had just closed down the archaeological site in an effort to prevent the spread of the coronavirus. Incidentally, that was the day Greece reported the first cases of the virus, so the country was in total panic mode. Bummed that we wouldn't have the opportunity to explore the city, which was dedicated to Zeus and his cult, we went to bed and hoped for a miracle.

Early the next morning, we were disappointed to find out that Olympia would indeed remain closed for the foreseeable future. Zeus was the god I felt least connected with; whereas all the other gods had a specialization and specific realm of influence, Zeus was always portrayed as simply the father of the gods. I knew there was more to him, and I had been looking forward to spending time meditating and receiving his energy.

Since we couldn't visit the temple, we spent some time walking around the fences and did a short meditation there. It somewhat helped me get in touch with Zeus's energy, but it left me yearning for more. Later that day, we packed up and headed for another long road trip back to Athens. Little did I know that Zeus had other plans for us. . . .

A few hours in, we found ourselves driving through tiny villages in the mountains on narrow dirt roads that were getting dangerously muddier from the heavy rains earlier that week. Google was taking us along the fastest route to Athens, but that meant crossing through what seemed like an endless mountain range. On a particularly muddy dirt road, in the middle of the mountains and miles away from the nearest village, we hit a dead end. We were faced with a pool of muddy water on a narrow road at the edge of a cliff.

I implored Sargis to head back and find an alternative route, but he insisted he could drive through it. Spoiler alert: he couldn't. He pressed on the gas to speed through the pool. The car sank into the mud and slid to the edge of the mountain to what could've been our deaths! We both screamed as the car finally came to a halt. Frozen with fear, I closed my eyes and called upon Zeus. "Zeus, thank you for helping us get out of here alive. Thank you for showing us the way."

Instantly, my shoulders relaxed and I let out a sigh of relief. I felt Zeus's energy saturate the air around us. It centered and grounded me, cleared my mind, and reassured me that it would all work out. And it did. I was guided to get out of the car, move some rocks out of the way, and create space for the car to turn around so that we could take an alternative route.

As soon as we made it out of the dirt road and back onto the paved street (I'd never been so happy to see asphalt!), we both sighed with relief. In that instant, an eagle flew right past our car and sat on a tree facing us. The eagle is Zeus's symbol and sacred animal, so I instantly knew it was Zeus making himself present. I looked the eagle in the eyes and smiled. "Thank you," I whispered. I might not have had the opportunity to *meet* Zeus at Olympia, but in that moment, I'd *known* him.

The Essence of Zeus

The root of Zeus's name is the Latin *deus* (god), *dies* (day), and the Greek *eudia* (fair weather). Zeus is the Sky Father who holds power over the weather and lightning. In fact, in Greece his name was so intertwined with the sky that in everyday life people would say, "Zeus is raining" rather than "It is raining." He is often portrayed as a warrior king holding a thunderbolt high in his right hand or on a throne with a scepter in hand.

From a mythological standpoint, Zeus is the king of the gods because he had to earn his rule through struggle and defend it against rebellion. According to his creation myth, before Zeus and the rest of the Olympians, Zeus's father and the other Titans ruled the world. Fearing a curse that one of his children would overthrow him, Kronos, who was married to Rhea, swallowed all his children as soon as they were born. Zeus was the last to be born, and to protect him Rhea gave Kronos a stone to swallow instead of Zeus, while sending Zeus to be brought up by an Oceanid nymph named Metis (Wisdom). Once he came of age, Zeus overthrew Kronos, freed his brothers and sisters, and defeated the Titans using his thunderbolts, establishing a new world order.

Zeus's overthrowing of the Titans, and the 12 Olympian gods' establishment of a new world order, is an allegory of the evolution of the cosmos and human consciousness through time. The first generation of the gods comprised Chaos, Gaia, and Eros, followed by the second generation of the 12 Titans, and then finally the third and fourth generations of the 12 Olympians. The myths surrounding the succession of the gods are simply a symbolic representation of the increasing refinement of human consciousness and world order.

From this perspective, Zeus isn't the creator of the cosmos or the Universe. As I explained in the first part of the book, the Universe simply *is*, and it's in a constant state of evolution and refinement. The gods, including Zeus, are the Universe's laws and functions. On a physical level, Zeus is the Sky Father, but not the sky itself (that's Ouranos). Instead, he oversees the various sky functions, such as cloud formations, rain, thunder, wind, and storms.

Zeus is also the representation of the Divine Masculine and his wife Hera the representation of the Divine Feminine. Zeus's energy acts like the divine semen that impregnates Hera's womb, the Earth, with new life. The physical functions that Zeus controls—the clouds, rain, thunder, wind, and storms—are some examples of the ways through which he creates new life on Earth. The rain, for example, can be imagined as Zeus's semen showering the Earth to give rise to new life, while the thunderbolt represents the creative, pollinating energy of the cosmos, the primal life force that enlivens all creation. So important was the thunderbolt in ancient Greece that it was honored as a god itself and has its own Orphic Hymn (see "Orphic Hymn to Zeus Keraunius—Zeus the Thunder," later in this chapter).

Zeus's Divine Masculine energy also manifests on a spiritual level. He transforms chaos into order, harmony, and balance and fends off any forces that seek to destroy this order. Essentially, Zeus holds the cosmos together and ensures that everything (including the gods and their functions) works as it should. Zeus is the totality of all cosmic systems and the divine intelligence that keeps everything together and working. He is the cosmos's etheric framework, so to speak.

Rather than being a monarchy, his rule is based on equality and collaboration. He doesn't impose his rule over the cosmos and the gods; rather, he maintains a commonly agreed and collaborative cosmic balance. In other words, he ensures that the cosmic structure that we all collectively agreed upon is sustained.

Whereas all 12 gods have a double role and presence in life, one relating to the physical cosmos and another relating to the soul's journey of ascension, Zeus is the one overseeing this system. As the father of the gods, he presides over the soul's journey of ascension, ensuring that both the gods and soul beings play their part in the ascension process.

As the overseer of Universal laws, Zeus is also the embodiment of fate (*eimarmeni* in Greek). Everything occurs according to his divine plan and intention, which is in alignment with the laws of the Universe, and is co-created with all of life. He's infinitely wise and all-knowing, which is why he's associated with divination. Although the art of divination is largely ascribed to Apollo, Apollo gets his answers from Zeus, who holds access to fate. Therefore, Zeus knows everyone's and everything's fate, because he's the representation of the collective intentionality behind the function of the Universe.

Rather than imposing fate, Zeus is instead aware of the soul contracts, arrangements, and agreements already in place by all of life and oversees the system from which these emerge. There are many historical accounts of Zeus sending divinatory signs through his elements of influence, such as the wind, storms, thunder, cloud shapes, and eagles. My encounter with the eagle in Greece was Zeus communicating that it wasn't my fate to die that day. The eagle acted as a reminder that I'm protected and guided on my path.

In essence, Zeus is the container that holds the cosmos together and ensures everything's in order. Not only does Zeus's formative energetic container create cosmic order, but it can also be used to create order at the national, city, and household levels. In ancient Greece, Zeus Herkeios and Zeus Ktesios were representations of Zeus protecting physical possessions and the household, while all city-state laws were attributed to Zeus, and the people who administered justice received their guidance from the god. As ancient Greek tragic poet Aeschylus proclaimed in one of his lost tragedies, "Zeus is aether, Zeus is earth, Zeus is sky, Zeus is everything and what is still higher than this."[1] This pretty match captures Zeus's essence.

Zeus's Virtues

Zeus's two main virtues that you can embody to follow your purpose and path to spiritual ascension are justice and orderliness.

Justice

The virtue of justice, or *dikaiosyne* in Greek, stems from the word *dike*, "judgment." Aside from Zeus, justice's main curators are the goddesses Nemesis, the goddess of retribution; Themis, the goddess who personifies justice, law, fairness, and divine order; and Dike, the goddess of fair judgment. This virtue is best defined as compliance with and impartial application of Universal and human laws. In plain words, justice is the appropriate manner of being and doing things from a physical and spiritual perspective.

From a physical standpoint, we need to examine justice on both a personal and a collective level. On a personal level, Plato says that justice is "the unanimity of the soul with itself, and the good discipline of the parts of the soul with regards to each other and concerning each other."[2] Therefore, justice is being in harmony with our soul's desires and essence so that we recognize our gifts and talents and follow them, rather than trying to be the best at everything. From this perspective, justice is about the fair distribution of our soul's resources, in the sense that we specialize in what we excel in and follow our unique life purpose. This is also what the economic terms *specialization* and *division of labor* are all about.

To better understand the virtue of justice on a personal level, we also need to look at what constitutes an *injustice*. Plato also defines justice as "the state that distributes to each person according to what is deserved."[3] When we treat other people in unjust ways for the purpose of satisfying our own interests, or when we purposely don't recognize or respect people's unique qualities and differences, we rid them of the opportunity to share their authentic selves. This interpersonal injustice can be seen as a form of violence, as it violates people's right to share their essence as freely and equally as we do.

Collective justice has to do with our responsibility to respect and comply with both the divine order of the cosmos as well as our commonly agreed civic laws. When we come to see ourselves as part of the collective, rather than outside of it, we become deliberate participants in creating collective justice and coexisting peacefully. From this state of alignment, we then act justly toward ourselves and others by standing up for what's just (and speaking out against what's unjust) and being active participants in maintaining world order.

From a spiritual standpoint, justice is a Universal law that maintains divine order in the cosmos and its various planes of existence, monitoring the gods and their Universal functions and thus determining the natural course of things. Rather than being manmade, it's a natural, Universal law that simply is. It's a virtue led by Zeus but that all gods, including Zeus, have to abide by so that the cosmos operates as it should. Socrates captured the importance of this virtue by stating that justice is the key to being one with the gods,[4] while Aristotle considered justice to be the ultimate virtue, including all other virtues.[5]

Orderliness

Zeus's second main virtue is *eutaxia*—being in and maintaining order. As I explained in Chapter 2, *cosmos* means jewel in Greek, because it's the part of the Universe that has acquired natural order, harmony, and beauty. Zeus is both the container and the framework that maintains this cosmic order. The virtue of orderliness is about recognizing and aligning with the order of the cosmos, so we can find it within us and then express it in our lives. Thus, this virtue is about transforming ourselves into human jewels, personal cosmos that are beautiful, balanced, and in order.

An easy way to nurture inner order is by witnessing the order in nature and the cosmos. Our planet has existed for approximately 4.5 billion years, whereas humans have been here only for 350,000 years. During this time, the Earth has developed powerful processes to flush out impurities and maintain her well-being. Simultaneously, the Earth and the planets in our universe all move in harmony and with mathematical accuracy with one another. The laws and functions that run our cosmos are stable, accurate, and in perfect order.

Being extensions of Source energy in the cosmos, we also share the divine order of the cosmos. When we consciously take the time to observe and recognize the order in nature, we attune to it and find it within ourselves, too. When we find our inner order, it informs the way we think, feel, and behave, and so our entire human expression is guided by our alignment with Source. From this perspective, nurturing inner order creates healthy thinking, feeling, and behaving.

Ascending with Zeus

The practices in this section will help you align with Zeus's qualities and embody his essence.

Activation Mantra

I am safe and protected.

Taking a moment to center and ground yourself, place both hands on your heart or extend your arms up to the sky, and repeat this affirmation a few times or for as long as it takes to feel its essence. Rather than just saying the words, focus on embodying each word and truly understanding the meaning of what you're saying. Employ all your senses so that you can see, feel, hear, smell, and taste the qualities of the mantra.

Ascension Journal Prompts

Take out your journal and let yourself free-write your answers to these questions. These are meant to help you explore Zeus's primary qualities in your life, creating opportunities for healing and growth:

- What's your life purpose? Let yourself freewrite the answer to this question for at least five minutes.

- What are your unique skills, talents, and abilities, and how can you develop them?

- Is it easy for you to let go of control and trust the Universe? How can you trust more?

- How can you practice justice in your relationships and in the world?

- What in your life needs reordering?

Connecting with Zeus Out in Nature

As the father of the gods, Zeus is present within everything and everyone. However, he's long been associated with the sky and weather, so you can most potently access him during various weather conditions. Personally, I love connecting with Zeus during thunderstorms. We're lucky to have frequent thunderstorms during the winter in Cyprus, and I love sitting by the window and connecting with their energy.

Although it'd be dangerous to roam around in nature during thunderstorms, it's generally safe and pleasant to do during ordinary showers. In the West, we do everything we can to avoid getting rained on, forgetting that it's just water. Yes, depending on where you live, rainwater may be contaminated, but if you get the chance to be out in nature somewhere where you know the water quality's safe, give yourself the opportunity to go out and enjoy the rain (without an umbrella!).

While you do so, visualize that the rain is Zeus's divine semen (I know, that's an unfortunate analogy!) that both cleanses your body and energy of what doesn't serve you and infuses you with spiritual vitamins and qualities that you can use to progress on your life purpose and ascension journeys. At the end of this practice and after you've dried yourself off, be sure to take out your journal and make a note of any new goals or desires that the rain may have imbued you with.

Orphic Hymn to Zeus

Use this ancient Zeus hymn whenever you need to deeply activate or call upon Zeus's presence. Ideally, stand straight, extend your hands up to the sky, and recite the hymn out loud.

> Much-honored Zeus, great god,
> indestructible Zeus,
> we lay before you in prayer redeeming testimony.
> O king, you have brought to light divine works—
> earth, goddess and mother,
> the hills swept by the shrill winds,
> the sea and the host of the stars,
> marshaled by the sky.
> Kronian Zeus, strong-spirited god,

the thunderbolt is your scepter,
father of all, beginning and end of all,
earth-shaker, increaser and purifier,
all-shaker, god of thunder and lightning,
Zeus the sower.
Hear me, god of many faces,
grant me unblemished health,
please grant me divine peace and riches,
please grant me glory without blame.

Orphic Hymn to Zeus Keraunius—Zeus the Thunder

Remember that Zeus's thunderbolt was honored as a god. The thunderbolt represents the divine light of creation, the life-force energy that flows within everything and everyone. Connecting with Zeus Keraunios will charge you with the energy and motivation you need to bring your desires and life purpose into life.

Father Zeus, sublime is the course
of the blazing cosmos you drive on,
ethereal and lofty the flash of your lightning
as you shake the seat of the gods
with a god's thunderbolts.
The fire of your lightning
emblazons the rain clouds,
you bring storms and hurricanes,
you bring mighty gales,
you hurl roaring thunder,
a shower of arrows.
Horrific might and strength sets all aflame,
dreadful missile makes hearts pound and hair bristle.
Holy and invincible,
it comes with a sudden crash,
an endless spiral of noise,
omnivorous in its drive,

unbreakable and threatening,
ineluctable, too, the gale's sharp
and smoke-filled shafts swoop down
with a flash dreaded by land and sea.
Wild beasts cringe when they hear the noise,
faces reflect the brilliance
of thunder roaring in the celestial hollows.
You tear the robe that cloaks heaven,
you hurl the fiery thunderbolt.
O blessed one . . .
the anger of the sea waves,
the anger of the mountain peaks—
we all know your power.
Enjoy this libation and give
all things pleasing to the heart:
a life of prosperity, queenly health,
divine peace that nurtures youths,
crowned with honors,
a life ever blooming with cheerful thoughts.

Zeus's Symbolism

As you feel guided, use the following to invite Zeus's essence into your home and sacred spaces. You can also use these symbols to set up a Zeus altar, as explained in Chapter 23.

- **Colors:** Deep red, deep purple
- **Symbols:** Thunderbolt, scepter, isosceles cross
- **Sacred animals:** Osprey, eagle, bull, lion, ram, sheep
- **Sacred plant/fruit:** Oak
- **Offerings:** Tokens of eagles, carnations, olive branch, styrax incense

Activation Meditation

Sit in a relaxed position, close your eyes, get into a meditative state using the Meditation Prep Process, and follow these steps to activate Zeus's energy within you:

1. Bring your attention to your crown chakra at the top of your head, and then become aware of the six other chakras aligned in the center of your body—your third eye, throat, heart, solar plexus, sacral, and root chakras. When you connect with the gods and the spiritual realms in general, you receive their guidance through your crown chakra and then the energy moves down through and is metabolized by your entire chakra system until it grounds from your root chakra into the Earth.

   When your chakras are cleansed and energized, this flow of energy allows you to receive and actualize divine guidance so you can know, follow, and fulfill your desires and life purpose. When your chakras are blocked, the energy doesn't flow freely through your chakra system, which creates obstacles and delays in your journey.

   Take a few deep breaths to observe the flow of energy from Source to your crown chakra and down through your entire chakra system. Use your mind's eye to scan this energetic flow and notice if there are any obstacles in the way.

2. Call upon Zeus's essence by affirming "I am Zeus" mentally or aloud. Using the "I am" affirmation is a powerful mantra for embodying the god's energy. While repeating this affirmation, you'll eventually feel Zeus's presence. You may see him with your mind's eye, feel his strength, or notice him through your other senses. Take a moment to acknowledge and welcome him.

   He stands strong with his right arm extended high, holding his mighty thunderbolt, his aura emanating a deep purple color while his divine eagle flies in circles around him.

3. Zeus offers to cleanse and activate your chakras and energetic line of communication with his thunderbolt, and you gladly accept. The thunderbolt holds the frequency of the divine energy of creation and has the ability to both cleanse and recalibrate the energy of anything it touches. Filling

yourself up with the thunderbolt's essence also awakens you to your purpose and gives you the wisdom and motivation to follow it.

Zeus points his thunderbolt up to the sky to activate the energy of divine thunder. Immediately, dark, rumbling clouds gather in the sky above you, charging up with powerful life-force energy. You're ready to receive it.

4. With intention, open your crown chakra and invite the thunder's energy to course through your body. Take a deep breath in and feel the thunder striking down from the booming clouds and into your body, following Zeus's guidance. Keep breathing deeply and let this divine electricity course through your seven chakras and entire body, clearing impurities, dissolving your fears and limiting beliefs, and aligning you to the energy of your life purpose and potential.

5. Once you feel cleansed and energized, take a few minutes to quiet your mind and meditate on your life purpose. With your energy cleansed and activated, you've raised your vibration to the vibration of your higher self. From this state, you have access to divine guidance as to your specific life purpose as well as the action steps you need to take to follow and fulfill it.

6. When the process feels complete, thank Zeus for this activation and gently wake up your body with small, slow movements. If you wish, take out your journal and use the journal prompts to channel more guidance, or make notes of the guidance you received during the meditation.

You can download an extended guided recording of this meditation at *www.GeorgeLizos.com/SOGM.*

CHAPTER 16

Demeter

In 2016 I was in my second year of working a corporate full-time job in London. The plan was to have a job that paid the bills while I developed my spiritual business part-time. That meant that after coming home from my 9 to 5 job, I'd start working on my own business until midnight, and then repeat the same cycle the following day. My weekends were also dedicated to my business, which meant that I had almost zero downtime to rest, recuperate, or have any kind of social life.

Although I received incessant signs from spirit to balance my life, I ignored them and kept on pushing . . . until one day that spirit decided to take hold of the situation. One morning, after a particularly long night working, I woke up intending to go to work, but my body wouldn't move. I'd burned myself out so much that my body went on strike. The Universe's message was loud and clear: I couldn't go on like this. Something had to change.

Desperate for balance but unaware of how to find it, I packed a weekend bag and headed for Glastonbury, a magical little village in the UK that had become my haven in times of crisis. In Glastonbury, I was led down a path of epiphanies and spiritual awakenings that completely transformed my life (you can read the full story in my book *Lightworkers Gotta Work*). During a particularly deep meditation on my last day there, I heard spirit's message clearly: quit your job, move back to Cyprus, and become self-employed. And that's what I did, in that order.

Fast-forward to the present moment, and my life has taken a 180-degree turn. I've finally found the balance between masculine and feminine energy; being productive and resting, growing and withering. But it wasn't an easy or instant process. Habits and routines take time to change, and I often relapsed to my workaholic tendencies. It wasn't until I actively started working with Demeter that I could solidify my new, healthier work/life routines.

Seeking to embrace both the masculine energy of creation and the feminine energy of rest, I set up an altar to both Demeter and Pluto, the god of the underworld. Every morning, I'd go to the altar, recite the hymn to the two gods, light a candle, and set an intention for balancing my masculine and feminine energy. Doing that first thing in the morning set the tone of my day and invited both gods to flow through me and guide the day.

Demeter and Pluto both reminded me that one cannot exist without the other. If the Earth's vegetation was in a constant process of growing and flourishing, the soil's nutrients would get depleted. Conversely, if nothing grew, the soil would become barren and lifeless. The cycle of blooming and withering is as essential to the Earth's well-being as it is to ours.

In truth, the two seemingly contrasting energies are actually two sides of the same coin. During the winter, the Earth may seem barren on the surface, but deep in the soil it's generating the nutrients for spring. Similarly, when plants flower in the spring and summer months, they continually release their younger form to embrace growth, until that eventually gives way and they return the nutrients back to the Earth. Demeter's daughter Persephone, who splits her time between Demeter's and Pluto's realms, is both the queen of the Underworld and the goddess of spring, embodying this balanced state.

The Essence of Demeter

Demeter is known as the goddess of the harvest, fertility, and agriculture. Her name comes from the Greek words *da* (earth) and *meter* (mother) and directly translates to Mother Earth. Demeter is, therefore, an earth goddess, but not necessarily the goddess of the earth. As I mentioned in Chapter 9, the goddesses of the earth are Gaia and Rhea, while Hera is the intermediary goddess between the earth and sky realms, giving life to everything inhabiting them and presiding over domestic life.

Demeter, on the other hand, represents the productive power of the Earth and the material world. She presides over the continuous expression of life on the planet, facilitating the unending cyclic nature of birth and rebirth that keeps the world running.

On a physical level, Demeter is a goddess of vegetation and agriculture, reigning over crops, grains, food, and the fertility of the Earth. Her son Plutus (not to be confused with Pluto, the god of the underworld), which literally translates to "wealth," represents the riches and abundance of the Earth. Her daughter Persephone represents the cyclic nature of the Earth with the changing of the seasons. Demeter's fertility also extends to human life, and she was often venerated as a goddess of birth, health, and marriage, which all require the goddess's motherly love and naturing qualities.

Demeter's essence and qualities are inherently tied with her daughter Persephone. Thus, to fully understand Demeter we need to understand Persephone's infamous abduction myth. According to the myth, the god of the underworld Hades/Pluto[1] was in love with Persephone and abducted her while she was casually gathering flowers one day, claiming her as his own. When Demeter found out her daughter was missing, she desperately searched for Persephone all over the world, during which nothing on the Earth could grow. Eventually, Helios, the god of the sun, told Demeter what had happened, and Zeus forced Hades to return Persephone to her mother. However, Hades tricked Persephone by giving her pomegranate seeds to eat, which tied her permanently to the underworld and she had to spend half the year with him.

The most obvious interpretation of the myth parallels Persephone's descent and ascent to Hades with the changing of the seasons, as well as the regeneration of life in the cycle of death and rebirth. The time Persephone spends in the underworld and Demeter's search for her signal the withering of the Earth during autumn and winter. Persephone's ascent to the Earth's surface and Demeter's joy at being reunited with her daughter mark the beginning of spring and summer. This is why Persephone is known as the queen of the underworld but also the goddess of spring and nature.

On a spiritual level, Demeter guides us to cultivate a virtuous life and nurture our souls along our ascension journey. In antiquity, the spiritual qualities of Demeter were celebrated during the Eleusinian Mysteries, spiritual initiations held yearly by the cults of Demeter and Persephone at Demeter's sanctuary in the ancient city of Elefsina, or Eleusis. Unfortunately, the procession of the Eleusinian Mysteries wasn't documented and has been kept secret, but from the few available sources we know that Persephone's myth was enacted as a way of guiding the initiates through the cyclic journey of life leading to the ascension of the soul.

The Eleusinian Mysteries were probably divided into three phases, representing Persephone's *descent* to the underworld, the *search* for her by Demeter, and Persephone's *ascent* to the Earth's surface and reunion with her mother. A possible spiritual explanation of the procession could be that Demeter represented the human soul and Persephone the soul lessons we learn along our reincarnation journey. The descent to the underworld, which is truly the material world we presently live in, represents our various life journeys of learning lessons and cultivating our souls, while Persephone's ascent represents our ascension to higher planes of existence.

Demeter's Virtues

Demeter's two main virtues that you can embody to follow your purpose and path to spiritual ascension are endurance and prudence.

Endurance

The virtue of endurance, or *karteria* in Greek, is about having strength, resilience, dedication, and persistence as we follow our dreams and purpose. It presupposes that we've taken the time to figure out what our life purpose is, come up with an action plan to follow it, and then taken conscious and consistent action toward it. *Endurance* is often used interchangeably with *patience*. In truth, while patience is a quality of endurance, pure patience is passive and endurance is more active and deliberate.

Endurance isn't about hustling, struggling, or exhausting yourself with action-taking. Instead, in the same way that the Earth goes through cycles of productivity and receptivity, endurance is about synchronizing ourselves with this cycle and finding that balance within us, too. The easiest way to embody this virtue is by observing and learning from the Earth's rhythms, which Demeter embodies. There are times in the year, month, week, and day that we're meant to be productive, and there's also a time for us to let go, surrender, and give our body the time it needs to recalibrate.

From this perspective, self-control is a subvirtue of endurance and has to do with our ability to monitor our action-taking and surrender on the way to following our purpose. Rather than consciously enforcing self-control through willpower and other external tools, we can instead align ourselves with it by connecting with the Earth's energy. By entraining ourselves to the rhythms of the Earth, we instinctively know how and when to monitor ourselves so we can take action without burning ourselves out. *Entrainment* is the practice of aligning one's vibrational frequency with the vibrational frequency of something else.

Another aspect of endurance is accepting and welcoming the discomfort that action-taking sometimes comes with physically, mentally, and emotionally. Plato defined this virtue as "endurance of labour for the sake of what is admirable." Oftentimes, mottos such as "no pain, no gain" and "great things come from hard work," allude to a toxic hustle mentality, but there's also truth to them when you see them from a different lens. Hard work can also be enjoyable work when it's aligned to our authenticity and life purpose. For example, writing this book is often mentally and emotionally tiring. It involves physical discipline, deep thinking, and emotional vulnerability. It *is* hard work, physically, mentally, and emotionally, but it's also totally worth it because it's aligned with my authentic self and purpose.

Endurance also has to do with embracing the so-called failures that come our way when following our purpose. Rather than seeing them as setbacks, we can instead recognize them as the Universe redirecting us toward a different path. Oftentimes, we think we know what the best course of action is for us, forgetting that there's a wiser plan already in place by the Universe, which knows exactly when and how to lead us to the next step on our journey. When pitching my book *Protect Your Light*, I tried for an entire year to find the perfect agent and publisher for it, to no avail. Eventually, I trusted that there was a higher plan already in place and surrendered. When the timing was right, everything aligned faster than I ever thought was possible, and the right agent and publisher showed up.

Prudence

The virtue of prudence, or *synesis* in Greek, requires steady, decisive, and deliberate movement toward what's right. To practice prudence, we first need to be aware of what it means to live a virtuous life, what our life purpose is, and the consequences of following it or not. Living a virtuous life is about embodying the gods' virtues to receive their wisdom, which then aligns us with our life purpose and the steps we need to take to follow it. Then, it's up to us to either use this information to take consistent action toward our life purpose or face the consequences of not doing so.

Beyond our life purpose, prudence has to do with our approach toward life in general, and the stance we have toward ourselves and other people. When we align with and practice prudence, we're better able to weigh in on things and place the right value on people and life's circumstances. Although we don't have control over other people's actions or what happens around us at any time, prudence affords us a higher perspective so we can see the hidden truths and deeper messages behind life's happenings.

To practice prudence, we need to find balance between our heads and our hearts. When we live life solely from a logical headspace, we shut down our intuitive channels and rid ourselves of the divine guidance that's constantly available to us. On the other hand, when we depend solely on our hearts, and therefore our emotions, we conflate instinctual urges and intuition and end up taking impulsive action steps, which look like intuitive guidance but really aren't. Instead, when we make decisions from a balanced head/heart space, we're truly tapping into divine guidance and taking the best course of action for us.

A great example of the distinction between head/heart decision and action-taking is how we decide what career to follow. If we depend solely on our head, and therefore logic, we follow the so-called proven, cookie-cutter, stereotypical pathways that society has carved out for us. Once we graduate from school, we often do some research on what types of careers are currently on the rise, choose one, and follow it, completely disregarding our natural talents, abilities, and desires. As a result, we end up doing jobs and living lives that look good on paper but deplete our hearts and souls.

On the other hand, when we depend solely on our hearts for making such decisions, we choose and follow what feels good in the moment without having a concrete vision or plan about how to move forward. People who make decisions only from their hearts end up moving from passion to passion and career to career. They never feel fulfilled and they restlessly search for the next shiny thing, hoping it'll give them the satisfaction they so desperately yearn for.

In my experience of working with spiritual seekers for more than 10 years now, I've noticed that most of them have lived life overdepending on their heads. Once they realize it's not working, they switch to the other extreme of depending solely on their hearts. As a result, they quit their soul-draining jobs and follow their passions. Because they hadn't taken the time to create an exit strategy and carve out a plan for the future, their leap of faith ends up in shambles, and they disappointedly regress to their head-based, soul-draining life.

Prudence offers an alternative. It guides us to consider both our heads and hearts when making decisions so that we take divinely guided action toward our dreams and purpose. In the example of choosing a career, the prudent thing to do would be to take our talents, abilities, and desires into account but also consider what logically makes sense for us to do given our life's circumstances, and then choose the sweet spot.

Ascending with Demeter

The practices in this section will help you align with Demeter's qualities and embody her essence.

Activation Mantra

I am attuned to the cyclic nature of life.

Taking a moment to center and ground yourself, place both hands on your heart or extend your arms up to the sky, and repeat this affirmation a few times or for as long as it takes to feel its essence. Rather than just saying the words, focus on embodying each word and truly understanding the meaning of what you're saying. Employ all your senses so that you can see, feel, hear, smell, and taste the qualities of the mantra.

Ascension Journal Prompts

Take out your journal and let yourself free-write your answers to these questions. These are meant to help you explore Demeter's primary qualities in your life, creating opportunities for healing and growth:

- What desires or areas of your life need more attention and nurturance?
- How can you find greater balance between rest and productivity?
- What aspects of yourself are in the process of withering, and what's ready to flourish?
- In what ways can you cultivate endurance?
- Have you mostly trusted your head, heart, or both?

Connecting with Demeter Out in Nature

My favorite way of connecting with Demeter out in nature is by meditating with and near trees. All plants, flowers, and especially trees have a connection to both the realm of the underworld and the realm of life. For this reason, trees have been utilized by many cultures and spiritual traditions for years as conduits for connecting with the spirit realms.

Pick a tree in your neighborhood or anywhere out in nature you feel an affinity with, sit on the ground with your back against its trunk, and close your eyes. Use the Meditation Prep Process to get into a meditative state, and then visualize yourself being as one with the tree's roots. Pay attention to the primarily feminine energy of rest and recalibration flowing through the roots and the Earth, at this level.

Continue by rising through the roots up the tree's trunk, all the way to the tree's branches and leaves. As you move upward, notice how the energy shifts from the relatively still energy of the undergrowth to the active, productive, masculine energy of the trunk, branches, and leaves. Allow yourself to become attuned to this energetic shift, noticing how it can also be true for you.

At the end of the meditation, take out your journal and make a note of the energetic shifts you experienced, noting any guidance you received about optimizing your lifestyle to experience this balanced state, too.

Orphic Hymn to Eleusinian Demeter

Use this ancient Demeter hymn whenever you need to deeply activate or call upon Demeter's presence. Ideally, stand straight, extend your hands up to the sky, and recite the hymn out loud.

> Deo, divine mother of all,
> goddess of many names,
> revered Demeter, nurturer of youths,
> giver of prosperity and wealth,
> you nourish the ears of corn,
> O giver of all,
> you delight in peace
> and in toilsome labor.
> Present at sowing, heaping, and threshing,
> O spirit of the unripe fruit,

you dwell
in the sacred valley of Eleusis.
Charming and lovely,
you give sustenance to all mortals;
you were the first to yoke
the ploughing ox,
the first to send up from below a rich,
a lovely harvest for mortals.
You are growth and blooming,
O illustrious companion of Bromios,
torch-bearing and pure,
you delight in the summer's yield.
From beneath the earth you appear,
gentle to all,
O holy and youth-nurturing lover
of children and of fair offspring.
You yoke your chariot
to bridled dragons,
round your throne
you whirl and howl in ecstasy.
You are an only daughter, but you have many children
and many powers over mortals;
the variety of flowers reflect
your myriad faces and your sacred blossoms.
Come, O blessed and pure one,
come with the fruits of summer,
bring peace,
bring the welcome rule of law,
bring riches, too, and prosperity,
and bring health that governs all.

Demeter's Symbolism

As you feel guided, use the following to invite Demeter's essence into your home and sacred spaces. You can also use these symbols to set up a Demeter altar, as explained in Chapter 23.

- **Colors:** Scarlet of the poppy, green, and earth tones
- **Symbols:** Sickle, torch, plough
- **Sacred animals:** Dove, bee, pig, sheep
- **Sacred plants/fruits:** Wheat, narcissus
- **Offerings:** Poppy, tokens of pigs, styrax incense, mint

Activation Meditation

Sit in a relaxed position, close your eyes, get into a meditative state using the Meditation Prep Process, and follow these steps to activate Demeter's energy within you:

1. Place both feet on the Earth. If you can, take off your shoes and socks and get outside so you have direct contact with the Earth. If it's not possible to do so, simply visualize that your feet are bare and touching the ground. Breathe deeply and take some time to connect with the energy of the Earth. Move your feet around if you can and notice the Earth's texture, temperature, and sound as you do so.

2. Call upon Demeter's essence by affirming "I am Demeter" mentally or aloud. Using the "I am" affirmation is a powerful mantra for embodying the goddess's energy. While repeating this affirmation, you'll eventually feel Demeter's presence. You may see her with your mind's eye, feel her strength, or notice her through your other senses. Take a moment to acknowledge and welcome her.

   She shows up in a long, white gown, holding a sheaf of wheat and wearing a fragrant flower wreath on her head. She radiates an earthy ochre light, and her smile emanates a sense of calmness and deep sense of knowing, which makes you feel at ease.

3. Demeter is here to help you align with the cyclic energy of the Earth. Walking closer to you, she takes off her flower garland and places it on your head,

attuning you to the Earth's frequency. As soon as she does that, you feel your feet growing roots and start digging down into the Earth.

4. Firstly, your roots expand outward at the surface of the Earth, connecting you to the various plants, flowers, and trees, which represent the most outward expression of the Earth's generating qualities. As you connect with the Earth's flora, let it awaken within you the same generating energy of expression and extroversion.

5. Secondly, your roots reach down into the Earth to connect with the multiple layers of soil in the Earth's crust. As your roots expand outward in all directions, you feel the breeding energy of this part of the Earth. Rich with minerals and bursting with life, this part of the Earth is in a constant motion of regeneration, breaking down dead matter and giving birth to new life. Let the energy course through your body and attune you to your own regeneration abilities.

6. As your roots dig farther down into the Earth, you reach various other layers of the Earth's crust, including rocks, caves, and crystals. These layers have more of a still, solid, and stable structure, yet they contain immense energy and potential for life. Allow your roots to connect with all kinds of rock and crystal energies, letting them fill up your body with their frequencies.

7. Your roots now reach the Earth's mantle and core, deep in the center of the planet. At more than 9,000 degrees Fahrenheit, the earth's core powers the entire planet. This energy is so powerful, both physically and energetically, that it can clear up almost any physical or energetic impurity on the planet. As you connect with the Earth's core, let its energy rise through your body to both cleanse and recalibrate your energy.

8. Spend some time in this state of interconnectedness with the planet, and let the balance of its masculine and feminine energy expand through your body, entraining you to it. Demeter surrounds you with her aura of earthly colored light, helping you assimilate the Earth's cyclic nature so you can express it instinctively in your life, as you follow your purpose and ascend on your soul's journey.

9. Before you come out of the meditation, bring both of your hands to your heart, and visualize your heart as a magnet drawing in the frequencies you've received from the Earth and Demeter's energy. Take a few deep breaths in and let your body adjust to this newfound, balanced state.

10. When the process feels complete, thank Demeter for this activation and gently wake up your body with small, slow movements. If you wish, take out your journal and use the journal prompts to channel more specific guidance, or make notes of the guidance you received during the meditation.

You can download an extended guided recording of this meditation at *www.GeorgeLizos.com/SOGM.*

CHAPTER 17

Hephaestus

The Temple of Hephaestus at the northwest side of the ancient Agora in Athens is one of the best preserved Doric temples in the area, as it remains largely intact. Sargis and I began our temple-hopping trip in Athens, so this was one of the first temples we visited. We were instantly captivated by it. There was an eerily serene energy at the temple's precinct—it felt as though we'd stepped into a portal of sorts. You could see that in other people's demeanor, too. As soon as they entered the vicinity of the temple, you'd see them slow down, breathe deeper, and be in the moment. I'll admit, I hadn't expected to feel so chilled out at a temple dedicated to Hephaestus, the god of fire, craftsmanship, and metal working. But I was soon to discover a whole new side of the god.

As we settled against a tree and prepared to meditate, we noticed wild tortoises roaming the temple's gardens. I didn't make much of it at the moment, but as I closed my eyes, breathed, and let Hephaestus take over, it all started making sense. I often thought of Hephaestus as this rough, limping god with a tired and crooked face, tirelessly forging metal tools I could never pronounce the names of. But the Hephaestus I experienced during my meditation was anything but. The serenity I'd felt walking around the temple was amplified, and the god's true colors and essence shone through.

The tortoises very much communicated the grounded creativity that Hephaestus is all about. In a hectic, patriarchal world that expects us to hustle 24/7,

Hephaestus invites us to slow down and take steady and consistent steps forward. I've always been impatient with everything in life, but especially with my creations. If I decide to do something, I throw myself in 110 percent and want to see results tomorrow. Yet this isn't always possible, which often leaves me feeling restless and frustrated.

Hephaestus taught me about the importance of consistency, timing, and gestation. As the god of fire and craftsmanship, Hephaestus is the king of manifestation. He understands that there are many factors to the creative process, some of which we can control and speed up, while others we have to accept and respect. Oftentimes, we wonder why our desires aren't manifesting as fast as we want them to, doubting ourselves and thinking there's something wrong with the process. But what if there's nothing wrong with ourselves or the process? What if it's just a matter of waiting for external factors to line up for our desires to manifest?

What's helped me understand this process in a felt way has been taking up craftmaking hobbies, specifically pottery. As much as I want to take home a ceramic mug the day I make it, I know there's a process I need to follow. First, I have to mold the clay into shape, wait for it to dry, sand it, fire it, glaze it, and fire it a second time. The whole process takes two to three weeks before it's done. However much I try to manifest my mug into being, it won't until the process is completed. The same is true for everything we create in life, whether it's a physical object, a digital creation, or any other type of manifestation.

Pottery not only has taught me to have patience when manifesting something but also has demonstrated the spiritual benefits of using my hands in the creative process. Although nowadays creation can take many forms, there's something sacred and grounding about making something with your own hands. Craftwork is ingrained into our energetic DNA, as it's something we've done for thousands of years. When we reignite that skill, we ignite our manifestation power and creative potential, which helps us move forward with our dreams and purpose. I can confidently say that since I got into pottery, I've been more consistent with and motivated to take action in other areas of my life, too.

The Essence of Hephaestus

In ancient Greece, Hephaestus was venerated as the god of fire, volcanoes, metallurgy, stone masonry, sculpture, technology, blacksmiths, artisans, and all sorts of craftsmen.

Today, he still presides over craftmaking but in a modern context. On a physical level, Hephaestus is behind the skill and manual work underlying all creations, whether tangible or intangible ones. Hephaestus directs the assembly of machinery and technological devices, the construction of buildings and cities, and any kind of creation that helps us evolve and live more efficiently. Hephaestus also guides the development of intangible technologies, such as software and AI technology. As Sargis said following our meditation at the Temple of Hephaestus, "Hephaestus turns a thought into something real. He turns something crude into something grand."

Hephaestus is distinguished from other Olympian gods by his close association with the element of fire. He is the embodiment of fire and also presides over it. In fact, his name is synonymous with fire; the two terms were often used interchangeably. Being fire, Hephaestus forms part of the four elements that make up the human body and all physical life. Energetically, Hephaestus joins forces with Aphrodite (who in this case stands for the element of earth and presides over the mingling of the elements to create new life), water, and air to create human life.

Consequently, at his essence Hephaestus is the creative fire of the Universe. He's everywhere you can find the element of fire, either physically or energetically. From a physical standpoint, Hephaestus is the life-force energy that creates and transforms things. He's the life-force energy of the Earth's physical processes (plate tectonics, volcanic eruptions, soil and rock formation, etc.), the natural world's biological functions (photosynthesis, metabolism, etc.), and the cosmos's planetary functions. From an energetic perspective, Hephaestus is the creative spark of our imagination, our epiphanies around new creations, and our drive for their manifestation. Whereas Athena looks after the strategy and framework behind creations, Hephaestus provides the life force that brings them to life.

In the same way that Hephaestus helps us build supportive technologies that contribute to our personal and collective evolution, he lends his creative fire to the other Olympians by smithing tools that help them fulfill their purposes. For example, Hephaestus forged Zeus's thunderbolts, Helios's chariot, Artemis's arrows, Hermes's Caduceus, Athena's aigis breastplate, Aphrodite's girdle, and Eros's bow and arrows.

As the god and embodiment of fire, Hephaestus is also at the beginning and end of cosmic paradigms. At the end of each cosmic period, when the world as we know it comes to an end, everything returns back to fire and provides the resources for the birth of a new cosmic reality. Hephaestus is the driving force behind these cosmic relaunches. In fact, the residents of the island of Lemnos, the center of the cult of Hephaestus, performed a purification festival to kindle new fire and distribute it to the island's craftsmen in honor of his transformative qualities.

Hephaestus's Virtues

Hephaestus's two main virtues that you can embody to follow your purpose and path to spiritual ascension are industriousness and resourcefulness.

Industriousness

The Greek virtue of *philoponia* is best translated as "industriousness" in English. As Plato puts it, industriousness is "the state which accomplishes what one has proposed . . . irreproachable state in respect of labour."[1] It is love for and a lifelong commitment to the work we do. Practicing this virtue means finding your purpose and taking daily and consistent action toward following and fulfilling it. It's the understanding that through zeal and diligent focus, we can complete any task and manifest any desire we set our mind to and achieve greatness. Although industriousness can certainly lead to riches and material gains, it's not necessarily tied to it; when we work solely for material gain without following a higher purpose, we run the risk of letting the ego, not our soul, guide the way.

The most important quality of industriousness is consistency. I believe that hard, consistent work will always beat talent, and this is something I emphasize to my students in my online psychic development program, *Intuition Mastery School*. I was never psychically "gifted" growing up, yet through daily, consistent work, I became a skilled and successful psychic healer. I've done so with many of my other interests, too, including singing, acting, and playing the guitar. Industriousness is about not letting the concept of talent limit us, and instead knowing that through focused work we can achieve anything we want.

That being said, industriousness requires that the work we do and the desires we choose to manifest are aligned with our life purpose and soul's journey of ascension. According to Greek philosopher Isocrates, "Strive with your body to be a lover of toil, and with your soul to be a lover of wisdom, in order that with the one you may have the strength to carry out your resolves, and with the other the intelligence to foresee what is for your good."[2] Therefore, being industrious isn't about doing work for the sake of it or following our ego's desires for material gains. Instead, it's about letting our soul communicate to our body the work we should be doing to follow our purpose and create positive change in the world.

Another component of industriousness, when utilized correctly, is risk-taking. Taking risks is a matter of getting out of our comfort zone and doing things that challenge us. Unless we do so we can't really grow, and unless we grow, we can't follow our purpose or achieve anything of substance. The reason many people are afraid of taking risks is because of the inevitable change and uncertainty that comes with it. Change is challenging. It brings up new factors to consider, limiting beliefs to release, and emotions to heal. Consequently, it's safer to remain the same, even if that means sacrificing joy and fulfillment.

To overcome the fear of taking risks, we need to heal our relationship with uncertainty. In fact, the quality of our life depends on the quality of our relationship with uncertainty. When we accept uncertainty, we start embracing risk-taking and the change it brings. Our embracing of risk-taking raises the level of our industriousness, in the sense that the work we do becomes increasingly challenging, and the subsequent growth, joy, and fulfillment we get from it multiplies. As Alexander the Great put it, "Toil and risk are the price of glory, but it is a lovely thing to live with courage and die leaving an everlasting fame."[3]

Practicing industriousness by following our purpose and doing things we love is a matter of self-respect. We've incarnated for the purpose of fulfilling a specific mission and contributing to our collective purpose of global positive change. Therefore, practicing industriousness is a matter of respecting the soul's—both our own and other people's—evolutionary journey and collective purpose. Unless we're active participants of our planet's ascension, we automatically contribute to its regression and destruction. If we're passive observers of life, we soon become energy vampires that rid the world of its life force, rather than adding to it.

Beyond a virtue we can practice, industriousness is a Universal law. When you look at the natural world and the Universe as a whole, you realize that it's in an unending process of evolution. Nothing is ever still; it's all constantly expanding, changing, and growing. As members of nature, it's important for us, too, to be part of this cosmic rhythm and contribute to its evolution, personally and collectively.

I'm currently doing my fifth college degree, and people keep asking me when I'll finally settle down. To me, settling down means stagnation and regression. If I stop learning, I stop growing. The ancient Greek tragedists, Aeschylus, Sophocles, and Euripides, wrote hundreds of books over the course of their lives. They deeply and fully committed to their craft and gave it everything they had. They didn't settle. Why should I? Why should you?

Resourcefulness

Stoic philosopher Chrysippus defined the virtue of resourcefulness, or *eumichania* in Greek, as "the science of finding the way out of things."[4] Specifically, resourcefulness is the conscious willingness and effort to come up with solutions. Such solutions may involve inventing new physical tools and immaterial systems, processes, and software or making improvements to existing ones.

Plato related resourcefulness to the virtue of *euporia*, "inventiveness," and defined it as having "good judgement which triumphs over something said."[5] Thus, he gave inventiveness and resourcefulness a different dimension by sharing how these virtues can be actively used in interpersonal relationships to resolve conflict and overcome doubts and hardships.

Although inventing new tools, practices, and solutions is an essential aspect of resourcefulness, it's only a virtue when they are within the realm of possibility and serve our personal or collective purposes. Wasting our time and energy trying to create something that goes against Universal laws, and is therefore impossible to create, isn't being resourceful but being misguided. Concurrently, inventions and solutions that don't support the common good, or actively seek to disrupt it—such as weapons, offensive military strategies, and criminal technologies—are all opposed to the virtue of resourcefulness.

Another quality of resourcefulness is effectively completing the invention at hand. However, there's a thin line between completing something and obsessing over perfecting it. Perfectionism is actually a disruptive force to inventiveness and resourcefulness rather than a supportive one, because it's rooted in personal neuroticism rather than a desire to create a solution. That's because time spent perfecting something that's already able to serve its intended purpose is time taken away from other projects and inventions.

Resourcefulness is about seeing the possibilities in seemingly impossible situations. The popular saying "there's always a choice" captures the essence of this point, as there are always multiple solutions to problems even if one seems impossible at the time. Resourcefulness is the skill of seeing beyond the surface and uncovering the choices and solutions that are always there. This tenacious aspect of resourceful-ness is what's responsible for the continuous inventiveness of the human race and the development of civilizations for thousands of years. Inventions considered impossi-ble in the past, such as electricity, flight, and the internet, are now taken for granted, because resourceful people didn't accept the status quo and sought to find solutions where there seemed to be none.

Ascending with Hephaestus

The practices in this section will help you align with Hephaestus's qualities and embody his essence.

Activation Mantra

I turn thoughts to things.

Taking a moment to center and ground yourself, place both hands on your heart or extend your arms up to the sky, and repeat this affirmation a few times or for as long as it takes to feel its essence. Rather than just saying the words, focus on embodying each word and truly understanding the meaning of what you're saying. Employ all your senses so that you can see, feel, hear, smell, and taste the qualities of the mantra.

Ascension Journal Prompts

Take out your journal and let yourself free-write your answers to these questions. These are meant to help you explore Hephaestus's primary qualities in your life, cre-ating opportunities for healing and growth:

- Make a list of your proudest creations.
- How can you optimize your creative process?
- In what ways can you make your work more enjoyable?
- How has your relationship with uncertainty changed over time?
- How can you be more resourceful when challenges come up?

Connecting with Hephaestus Out in Nature

As the god of physical fire but also the spiritual, energetic fire of creation, Hephaestus can be experienced anywhere and everywhere fire manifests in the world. Ideally on a sunny day, go for a walk out in nature or even in your neighborhood (Hephaestus's energy, like fire, manifests in all life, including urban spaces).

Start your walk by being mindful of how fire manifests within your own body. Feel the warmth of your body as your heart circulates the blood, notice how your breath warms up in your lungs while you breathe it in, and become aware of how your body's biological processes are utilizing fire to perform their various functions. Furthermore, appreciate your brain for utilizing energetic fire to think, process information, and come up with creative ideas.

Gradually expand your awareness to the world around you and think about how fire manifests in the space around you. How does fire manifest in the pavement you walk on, the buildings you're surrounded by, and the technology you and other people use? What role does fire play in the natural world? Besides the obvious sources of fire, such as the sun and other open fires, notice the fire driving photosynthesis and other biological processes within plants, trees, and all vegetation. Think about how fire manifests in the ground below you. The processes that produce soil, rock, and crystal formations underground all utilize fire created from friction, pressure, and the Earth's mantle.

Finally, end your walking meditation by considering how the intelligent, creative fire of Hephaestus works on a spiritual level. The intentions, thoughts, emotions, drive, and creativity that created us, our planet, and the cosmos are all expressions of Hephaestus's creative fire in action. Take a moment to appreciate the scale and power of this divine fire, and set the intention of channeling it in your life and purpose moving forward.

Orphic Hymn to Hephaestus

Use this ancient Hephaestus hymn whenever you need to deeply activate or call upon Hephaestus's presence. Ideally, stand straight, extend your hands up to the sky, and recite the hymn out loud.

> *Hephaistos, powerful and strong-spirited,*
> *unwearying fire,*
> *shining in the gleam of flames,*
> *a god bringing light to mortals,*
> *mighty-handed,*

eternal artisan,
worker, part of the cosmos,
blameless element,
most sublime, all-eating,
all-taming, all-haunting—
ether, sun, stars,
moon, pure light:
all these parts of Hephaistos
are revealed to mortals.
All homes, all cities,
all nations are yours.
O mighty giver of many blessings,
you dwell in human bodies.
Hear me, lord, as I summon you
to this holy libation,
that you may always come
gentle to joyful deeds,
end the savage rage
of untiring fire
as nature itself
burns in our own bodies.

Hephaestus's Symbolism

As you feel guided, use the following to invite Hephaestus's essence into your home and sacred spaces. You can also use these symbols to set up a Hephaestus altar, as explained in Chapter 23.

- **Color:** Red
- **Symbols:** Fire, hammer, anvil, axe, copper, bronze
- **Sacred animals:** Dog, donkey, crane
- **Sacred plant/fruit:** Pine tree
- **Offerings:** Daisies, frankincense incense

Activation Meditation

Sit in a relaxed position, close your eyes, get into a meditative state using the Meditation Prep Process, and follow these steps to activate Hephaestus's energy within you:

1. Visualize yourself at Sicily's Mount Etna volcano, where, according to myth, Hephaestus had his divine workshop. Walk up the volcano's side and stand at the edge of the crater, looking down into the bubbling lava. Breathe in, open your arms to the sides, and let the energy of the thick fumes and the scorching heat cleanse your body and aura of all toxic and negative energies.

2. Call upon Hephaestus's essence by affirming "I am Hephaestus" mentally or aloud. Using the "I am" affirmation is a powerful mantra for embodying the god's energy. While repeating this affirmation, you'll eventually feel Hephaestus's presence. You may see him with your mind's eye, feel his strength, or notice him through your other senses. Take a moment to acknowledge and welcome him.

   Hephaestus rises up from the depths of the volcano to greet you. He sports a short beard, wears a surprisingly clean short chiton (tunic) and an oval metallic cap, and holds his infamous hammer. His aura emanates a fiery red light that invigorates everything it touches.

3. Hephaestus invites you to take a trip with him through the volcano to the depths of the Earth. Holding hands, you jump together into the crater and dive deep into the lava. Your first stop is Hephaestus's workshop, where he and the other fire elementals forge the divine tools that the gods use to run the cosmos. As you look around the workshop, you appreciate the intricate mechanics and divine intelligence that flows through the cosmos, ensuring that everything works according to plan and in perfect order.

4. As you leave Hephaestus's workshop, you cross the threshold of the Earth's crust and into the deep magma. Through powerful convectional currents, the magma moves the Earth's tectonic plates, generating earthquakes and volcanic eruptions that, although destructive for humans, are necessary for cleansing and revitalizing the planet, both physically and energetically.

5. Finally, Hephaestus guides you to the Earth's inner core at the center of the planet, which you can visualize as a giant ruby-colored crystal ball. The inner core is to the Earth what the sun is to our galaxy. It's the Earth's powerhouse that drives life on, below, and above the Earth. Spend some time meditating within the Earth's core and let yourself align with its frequency. This is the purest frequency of Hephaestus's creative fire, which you can also use to manifest your desires and purpose.

6. To complete your activation, Hephaestus gifts you his divine hammer, the ultimate symbol of creation. As you hold it, its energy courses throughout your entire body and being and activates the creative potential of every atom within you. While this energy is being activated, allow yourself to ponder your desires, purpose, and manifestations. Let the frequency of creation ignite your passion and motivation for taking action to turn things from thoughts to reality.

7. When the process feels complete, thank Hephaestus for this energetic activation and travel with him back up through the Earth's mantle and the lava, exiting the crater at Mount Etna. Gently wake up your body with small, slow movements and come out of the meditation feeling great! If you wish, take out your journal and use the journal prompts to channel more specific guidance, or make notes of the guidance you received during the meditation.

You can download an extended guided recording of this meditation at *www.GeorgeLizos.com/SOGM.*

CHAPTER 18

Ares

A res, the Greek god of war, is one of the most, if not *the* most, misinterpreted of the 12 Olympians. Often depicted as a brusque, armored warrior on a chariot harnessed by his sons Phobos (Fear) and Deimos (Terror), he's been painted as a brutal, destructive, and dangerous god.

Often, when I tell people I practice Greek paganism, I'm met with flabbergasted faces, as they wonder how I can teach about love and spirituality while believing in gods that lead wars and drive destruction, using Ares as an example.

I'll be honest, I asked myself the same question when I first transitioned to Greek paganism. Although I understood that the mythological portrayal of the gods was allegorical and the gods were loving and pure in nature, I still couldn't understand how that could be the case for a god of war.

Yet, while meditating and connecting with the essence of Ares at the Temple of Ares in the ancient Agora in Athens, I received a starkly contrasting energetic impression of the god. Instead of fear, rage, and terror, the emotions most often associated with Ares, I felt a deep sense of peace coupled with unbridled trust in myself and an urge to take fearless action forward.

In the next couple of years, I dived into the cult of Ares's worship in ancient times, studied the various philosophical texts about his qualities, and meditated with him. Finally, the true essence of the god of war was revealed to me, and it all made sense.

The Essence of Ares

Ares is known as the god of war and courage. His name comes from the Greek word *ara*, meaning curse and ruin. Rather than simply the god of war, Ares is the god of all conflict, and he was called upon only when all other options were exhausted and there was no peaceful way forward.

He represents the blind, raw expression of energy that's often characterized by rage, aggression, unbridled passion, and courage. His energy is wild, unruly, loud, and unrefined. Ares's energy overpowers most other powers, apart from Athena's wisdom, strategy, and prudence, which shows the superiority of wisdom over force.

Going back to my earlier point, one could argue that there's not much love in Ares's combative nature. Yet sometimes the most loving thing you can do, for others or for yourself, is fight.

Although we're physical extensions of the Universe and share the gods' inherent purity and loveliness, we're also in a physical world that allows for disconnection from our true nature. We've consciously chosen to incarnate in a world of polarity, in which people are free to maintain or neglect their alignment with their higher selves. When people disconnect from their true nature and shift toward their egos instead, conflict may be the only way forward to protect ourselves.

A common expectation of spiritual people is to continually maintain a state of peace, love, and high-vibe energy. We're pressured to think positively 24/7, not feel negative emotions, see the higher perspective in all situations, never engage in conflict, and therefore, repress or deny our ego at all costs. In my experience, repressing these natural human states often results in self-victimization, spiritual bypassing, and toxic positivity, rather than the loving and spiritual experience we'd hoped for.

A clear example of this is many of my clients' response when they're on the receiving end of a verbal or even physical attack: "I just send them love and light and hope they find their way." What's problematic about sending love and light to people who attack us is that our love and light doesn't really correct their action. It enables it.

What Ares has helped me understand is how important it is to bounce between my higher self and ego, depending on the circumstances. If we were meant to be love and light at all times, we wouldn't have incarnated on this planet in the first place. Instead, we've chosen to exist on a planet that allows for contrast and polarity, with the purpose of using that and learning to play by its rules.

This doesn't mean allowing ourselves to descend into ego, but instead maintaining our connection with our higher selves so we can manage and employ our ego when we have to. In the case of conflict, there's little our love and light can do when we're under physical, verbal, or energetic attack. Instead, in these cases our ego— in the form of the physical body, words, and energy—is our most powerful tool for protection.

Examples of personal situations when direct conflict may be the most loving course of action include verbal or physical attack, bullying and harassment, domestic or sexual abuse, or any other instance in which our physical or other boundaries aren't being respected.

On a collective level, sometimes conflict in the form of war is the most loving way forward, too. Aristotle puts forth a great justification for this as part of the *just war theory*, which originated in ancient Greece: "The proper object of practising military training is not in order that men may enslave those who do not deserve slavery, but in order that first they may themselves avoid becoming enslaved to others."[1]

Taming Ares

Aside from Ares's combative nature, the ancient Greeks often utilized his blended energy with goddess Aphrodite. According to myth, Aphrodite's favorite lover was Ares, with whom she had several children, including the goddess Harmonia, meaning harmony or concord. This allegorical story demonstrates that only love can overpower conflict and bring peace and harmony. Therefore, the union of the two gods and their energies is the solution to ending conflict and restoring peace.

Another example of taming Ares's combative energy to bring peace is found in his chained statues in Sparta and various cities in Anatolia. The cities, often under threat from pirates in the late Hellenistic era, were given an oracular instruction to build and ritually chain down statues of Ares as a way of bringing and maintaining peace. As the oracle proclaimed, "thus will he become a peaceful deity for you, once he has driven the enemy hoard far from your country, and he will give rise to prosperity much prayed for."[2]

This oracular proclamation, along with the merging of Ares's and Aphrodite's energies, gives an important dimension to Ares's sphere of influence. In the short term, we need his raw combative nature for protection and restoring peace. In the long term, the most sustainable way of restoring peace is by proactively nurturing inner and outer peace.

Ares's Virtues

Ares's two main virtues that you can embody to follow your purpose and path to spiritual ascension are bravery and courage. Although these two terms are often used interchangeably in English, they have key distinctions in Greek.

Bravery

The Greek term for bravery is *eupsychia*, which comes from the Greek word *psyche*, "soul." Therefore, bravery is a virtue and quality of the soul. It's the state of inner balance and personal freedom that comes from being in alignment with our souls and authentic selves. It stems from deep awareness of our true nature, life purpose, and the responsibility to follow it. It's the urge to freely and fearlessly share our unique expression with the world.

Bravery isn't connected with the ego's desire to be seen, prove oneself, or overshadow others; rather, it draws from the understanding of our true essence and the irrepressible need to express it. Therefore, bravery isn't a selfish, ego-based virtue, but instead a social one. It's the energy that drives us to make the world a better place. Bravery asks us to see beyond our personal well-being, embrace the true qualities of our soul and purpose, and channel them with the aim of creating collective positive change.

Bravery is one of lightworkers' most important virtues to nurture. In my book *Lightworkers Gotta Work*, I coined the term *ascension lightworkers*. These are old, mature souls who incarnate on the planet time and time again in order to make the world a better place. Bravery calls for lightworkers to see beyond just their personal well-being and desires, and instead focus on creating change on a global scale.

When we connect with our souls through our spiritual practice, the ego's hold on us gradually softens and we're able to clearly know our life purpose and how to go about fulfilling it. When we come into this state of alignment, we instinctively shift from solely selfish desires and realize the collective dimension of our presence and purpose. This doesn't mean denying our ego or our personal desires, but rather expanding our awareness to take the collective into consideration, too.

Courage

If bravery is being in alignment with our authentic self so we can realize and accept our life purpose, then courage, or *tharalleotita* in Greek, is the physical, mental, and emotional strength required to follow it. Therefore, bravery is a virtue of the soul and courage a virtue of the body and mind, and the two work in tandem to guide our ascension journey.

Courage is often misinterpreted as risk-taking, such as trying a dangerous sport or activity, or thrill-seeking, such as setting high-stakes goals for ourselves. Although courage does involve a sense of risk or thrill, it's got more to do with overcoming the resistance that prevents us from expressing our soul's qualities and following our life purpose. Sometimes this resistance is internal (in the form of fears, traumas, and limiting beliefs), while other times the resistance is external (in the form of familial and social backlash to our actions).

To overcome internal resistance, we need to employ courage by doing the untangling work of identifying and healing our fears, traumas, and limiting beliefs but also doing the creative work of cultivating new, supportive thoughts, beliefs, and emotions. It's about embracing both practices—releasing the obstacles of the past and building new foundations—as fully and boldly as needed to follow and fulfill our purpose.

The more we undertake these practices, the more confident we eventually feel about ourselves and our purpose, and the less we're affected by the external resistance to our purpose, whether rejection, familial and social judgment, or other disappointments.

Cultivating alignment with our soul as a result of practicing bravery and courage also acts as a guiding force to using conflict mindfully. Our alignment gives us perspective in any situation, allowing us to make the right judgment calls and utilize the appropriate communication style. The absence of these two virtues can result in abusing Ares's energy by overdepending on the ego, which inevitably leads to destruction. Sadly, human history is rife with examples of people and countries abusing Ares's combative nature for ego-based purposes, rather than using it as a force for good.

Ascending with Ares

The practices in this section will help you align with Ares's qualities and embody his essence.

Activation Mantra

I stand up for myself and others.

Taking a moment to center and ground yourself, place both hands on your heart or extend your arms up to the sky, and repeat this affirmation a few times or for as long as it takes to feel its essence. Rather than just saying the words, focus on embodying each word and truly understanding the meaning of what you're saying. Employ all your senses so that you can see, feel, hear, smell, and taste the qualities of the mantra.

Ascension Journal Prompts

Take out your journal and let yourself free-write your answers to these questions. These are meant to help you explore Ares's primary qualities in your life, creating opportunities for healing and growth:

- What has been your relationship with conflict with others and within yourself?
- When has fighting been the most loving action you could take?
- How have other people's opinions prevented you from expressing your authentic self?
- How does your life purpose contribute to the ascension of the planet?
- In what ways can you be more courageous when following your purpose?

Orphic Hymn to Ares

Use this ancient Ares hymn whenever you need to deeply activate or call upon Ares's presence. Ideally, stand straight, extend your hands up to the sky, and recite the hymn out loud.

(Remember that this hymn was written at a time when Ares was primarily venerated as a war god, hence the references to blood and killing. If these terms are trigger-
ing or don't resonate, feel free to replace them with equivalent alternatives that apply
to your life's context, or to omit them completely.)

> *Unbreakable, strong-spirited, mighty and powerful daimon,*
> *delighting in arms, indomitable, man-slaying, wall-battering;*
> *lord Ares, your is the din of arms, and ever bespattered with blood*
> *you find joy in killing and in the fray of battle, O horrid one,*
> *whose desire is for the rude clash of swords and spears.*
> *Stay the raging strife, relax pain's grip on my soul,*
> *and yield to the wish of Kypris and to the revels of Lyasios,*
> *exchanging the might of arms for the works of Deo,*
> *yearning for peace that nurtures youths and brings wealth.*

Ares's Symbolism

As you feel guided, use the following to invite Ares's essence into your home and
sacred spaces. You can also use these symbols to set up an Ares altar, as explained in
Chapter 23.

- **Color:** Red
- **Symbols:** Steel weapons, lighted torches, shield, spear, helmet
- **Sacred animals:** Cock, dog, vulture
- **Sacred plant/fruit:** Poppy
- **Offerings:** Weapons, swan images, frankincense incense

Activation Meditation

Sit in a relaxed position, close your eyes, get into a meditative state using the Meditation Prep Process, and follow these steps to activate Ares's energy within you:

1. Visualize yourself standing at the edge of a vast, deep forest. Facing you is a
   long, winding path that stretches into the woods, promising a challenging
   but exciting journey. Think of this path as the journey to following your

life purpose, and you're the hero ready to do what it takes to reach your destination.

2. While standing there facing the path ahead, call upon Ares's essence by affirming "I am Ares" mentally or aloud. Using the "I am" affirmation is a powerful mantra for embodying the god's energy. While repeating this affirmation, you'll eventually feel Ares's presence. You may see him with your mind's eye, feel his strength, or notice him through your other senses. Take a moment to acknowledge and welcome him.

He's dressed in his usual attire, wearing steel armor; holding a shield in one hand and a spear in the other; and being carried by a war chariot. He stands tall and fearless, emanating a sense of strength, readiness, and authority.

3. As he gets off his chariot, he walks toward you, faces you, and points his etheric spear toward your root chakra. Your root chakra, found at the base of your spine, looks like an energetic ball of bright red light. It holds your primal sense of survival, protection, and security; therefore, it helps you courageously show up for yourself and others in life and on your ascension journey.

As he touches your root chakra with his spear, he activates the red ray within your root chakra that clears and activates it. This red beam of light saturates your root chakra, cleansing it from doubt, fear, and cowardliness, and restores it to its optimal state. Breathe deeply during the clearing and activation, letting the energy from your root chakra expand through your body and aura, infusing you with a sense of courage, protection, and security.

4. With your root chakra cleared and activated, Ares proceeds with dressing you in energetic armor, preparing you for the journey ahead. He carefully places a helmet on your head, a breastplate around your chest, and greaves for shin protection. Finally, he hands you a sword or a spear and a steel shield. Each piece of your armor holds energetic frequencies that instill within you bravery, courage, and the various Ares qualities that you need to protect yourself and others and to follow your purpose fearlessly. Once

you're fully dressed in your warrior attire, take a few deep breaths in and notice how it makes you feel.

5. Ready for the path ahead, express your gratitude to Ares and ask him to stay with you and guide your journey forward. Gently wake up your body with small, slow movements and come out of the meditation, feeling fierce!

You can download an extended guided recording of this meditation at *www.GeorgeLizos.com/SOGM.*

CHAPTER 19

Artemis

On the fifth day of our temple-hopping trip, Sargis and I visited the Temple of Artemis at the Asclepieion of Epidaurus, the most important healing sanctuary dedicated to the Greek god of medicine, Asclepius. Like her twin brother, Apollo, Artemis has been associated with healing, good health, and ritual purification, and it didn't take me long to witness that myself.

In most temples we'd visited thus far on our trip, it would take me a while to find the right energetic spot to sit and meditate. After taking some time to center, ground, and connect to the energy of each temple and its associated god, I'd start receiving claircognizant impressions and messages and sometimes short, spontaneous visions. This wasn't the case at the Temple of Artemis, where I had one of the deepest meditation healing journeys I've experienced so far.

As soon as I closed my eyes, I went into a semitrance state and was transported to a remote, mountainous forest. In my vision, I was completely naked and felt totally in sync with the natural world around me. I felt as one with the plants, flowers, trees, animals, wind, and sun, and was grateful to be in their presence. The forest felt like a home I hadn't known I'd had, and the plants and animals like a family I hadn't known I'd lost.

Most importantly, I felt totally at peace and in love with my body. All the judgment I'd previously had about my weight and my self-perceived physical imperfections had disappeared, and I was finally able to witness the miracle that I was. As my vision progressed, I saw myself running naked in the forest at night, howling with the wolves under the full moon, and harmonizing to the melodic song of the nightingales.

I came out of the meditation feeling recalibrated and seeing myself, and the world, with new eyes. *This is who Artemis is*, I thought. She's the love I felt toward my body. She's the raw, wild, instinctual energy I felt while running carelessly in the woods. She's the light of the full moon, the song of the nightingales, and the howls of the wolves. She's the unrefined, unbridled, and unapologetic Divine Feminine energy in nature, and in all of us.

That's when it hit me: I craved that energy. Living in a city and busying myself with all kinds of activities, I'd neglected my time in nature. I'd consciously left the corporate world in London and moved to Cyprus so that I'd spend more time out in nature, and yet I'd simply replicated my busy London life in a new city. Taking this journey with Artemis reminded me of the power of nature to restore and inspire us, which helped me recommit to Artemis, nature, and myself.

The Essence of Artemis

Artemis represents the raw, wild, virgin aspects of nature, and all things. She channels the primal, unbridled, and unruly qualities of the Divine Feminine, which is why she was imagined to live in wild forests untouched by humans. On a physical level, she's the protector of wild nature, presiding over trees, plants, flowers, and wild animals. Her epithet *Potnia Theron* literally translates to "Queen of Animals," as she was the mistress of all animals in the wild—fish, birds, reptiles, mammals, and amphibians.

On a spiritual level, Artemis's raw, wild, and virgin characteristics denote the purity of the perfected, enlightened souls at the final stages of their reincarnation journeys. Therefore, Artemis reminds us of and helps us connect with the true essence of our souls. She reminds us that when we let go of the ego's illusory perspectives of ourselves and of life, we automatically align with the pure and loving frequency of the Universe, and therefore, of ourselves.

As a child nurturer, or *kourotrophos*, Artemis is one of the goddesses guiding souls toward the final stages of their ascension journeys; this is why she had a temple at the Eleusinian Mysteries. Her mythological presence in wild forests and on mountain peaks is symbolic of the planes of spiritual height and purity she inhabits, and the planes that old, mature souls enter following their reincarnation cycle. She's often associated with the moon because it is at the Earth's outer auric layer, the dimension of the spiritual plane of existence where Artemis often resides.

Artemis is the goddess of hunting and of hunters. As the Queen of Animals, she's often portrayed as a huntress surrounded by deer, bears, and other forest animals. The animals accompanying Artemis symbolize the mature souls that she guides along their ascension journey. In mythological representations she is usually depicted holding a bow and silvery arrow, symbolizing various aspects of her essence. Shooting people with them is akin to gifting them her spiritual frequencies and attuning them to her purity.

Artemis is the twin sister of Apollo. According to the myth, Artemis was born first and then helped her mother Leto give birth to Apollo. The allegory behind this myth gives us an important lesson for spiritual ascension. Artemis symbolizes the purity, and Apollo the light, of our souls. Therefore, the myth demonstrates that our primary objective on our ascension journey is to align with the purity of our souls, and once we do so we're gifted with Apollo's light, which represents the divine guidance we need to move forward.

Artemis is also known as the protector of women and childbirth. Specifically, we often find Artemis in women's life transitions, such as in puberty, coming of age, childbirth, and transition to the afterlife. One of the reasons Artemis is so closely connected to the liminal stages of women's lives is because these are the phases during which women express the raw and pure energy of their souls. The unruly spirit of puberty, the liberating experience of losing one's virginity, the wild nature of childbirth, and the surrender that comes right before our transition all channel the untamed energy of the goddess.

Another reason we find Artemis in transitions is because as the goddess most interested in the evolution of our souls, she's also interested in the evolution of our current, physical life. Thus, like a caring mother Artemis helps us enter the world and then accompanies us through the main transitions of our lives until we pass and transition to the next stage of our evolutionary journey.

Artemis's Virtues

Artemis's two main virtues that you can embody to follow your purpose and path to spiritual ascension are temperance and self-control.

Temperance

The virtue of temperance, or *sophrosyne* in Greek, is about living life and taking action in a logical, balanced, and sound-minded way. Plato defined temperance as balancing our instinctive desires for pleasure with rationality.[1] Demophilus, a Pythagorean philosopher, described it as "the light of a soul free of disturbing passions."[2] Stoic philosopher Marcus Aurelius had a more practical explanation of temperance, calling it "the restraint of the appetites."[3] Cicero defined it as moderateness, modesty, and frugality.[4] Finally, in Euripides's tragedy *Hippolytus*, temperance, represented by Artemis, is defined as being pure, clear-headed, and untainted by sexual desire.[5]

At first glance, temperance feels like a restrictive virtue wanting to rid us of our desires and the pleasures of life. This couldn't be further from the truth. Instead, temperance is about finding alignment with our soul's essence and purpose, and then letting that alignment guide our desires and action-taking. Thus, temperance is not about keeping ourselves from enjoying life, but rather knowing what will truly help us enjoy life and going about it in a conscious way.

Aligning with nature and her laws is the easiest way to find alignment with our soul's essence and purpose. As Greek philosopher Heraclitus wrote, "sophrosyne is the greatest virtue, and wisdom is speaking and acting the truth, paying heed to the nature of things."[6] This means that temperance is found in and freely given to all by nature, as long as we take the time to align with her.

In ancient times, people lived in communities that respected and incorporated nature into daily life. Religion, civic life, and the urban environment were all integrated into the natural world rather than imposed on it. We can see this most potently by comparing the architecture of religious buildings in ancient and modern times. Ancient Greek temples were built in a way that reflected the harmony between humans and nature, while modern churches and cathedrals impose on nature to show the grandeur of a god that's external to it. As a result, the ancients were able to more easily maintain their alignment with nature, and therefore with their soul's essence and purpose.

Increasingly, people have distanced themselves from the natural world; we now live in megacities far removed from nature. In fact, according to one recent report, most Americans spend more than 10 hours per day in front of screens.[7] Other studies have found that people in North America and Europe spend at least 90 percent of their time indoors.[8] Our increasing disconnection from nature has resulted in a disconnection from our souls' authentic nature, too. We've lost touch with what truly fulfills us and are on a hamster wheel of constantly searching for rush, pleasure, and adrenaline.

Temperance is about restoring our connection with the Earth and subsequently with our souls so that we can enjoy the pleasures of life without overindulging or abusing ourselves. When we do so, we finally find the fulfillment we seek because the desires and pleasure we're instinctively guided to engage in reflect our souls' essence.

Self-Control

The virtue of self-control, or *enkrateia* in Greek, directly translates to "in power." Thus, self-control is about being in a state of power over something, usually our own urges and desires. The opposite of *enkrateia*, according to Aristotle, is *akrasia* (without power), which describes a lack of control over one's desires.[9] Someone who effectively practices self-control is conscious of what action steps will have positive consequences for them and others, while someone who lacks self-control takes impulsive actions that have negative consequences.

Thus, a key quality of self-control is the conscious awareness of the reasons for and consequences of practicing it. Practicing self-control because we know we must or feel obliged to isn't a virtue, it's coercion. However, when we consciously practice self-control because it's an extension of our values and authentic nature, then it becomes a tool for self-mastery—something we do deliberately to create a positive change for others and ourselves.

To understand the difference between practicing the virtue of self-control authentically versus doing so out of obligation, consider the stance that certain spiritual traditions take toward the ego. The ego is the part of ourselves that represents our physicality and personality, in contrast to the spiritual part of ourselves that's our soul and essence. Many spiritual traditions actively bash the ego, guiding students through practices to deny, repress, or surpass it. Doing so is practicing self-control out of obligation, and has nothing to do with the Greek virtue. Contrastingly, self-control isn't about repressing the ego but about acknowledging, respecting, and letting it express itself, as long as we don't let it take control. The key distinction here is maintaining alignment with our soul such that the soul is the one making decisions while also monitoring the ego and using it consciously to enjoy the pleasures of life.

Once we embrace the virtue of self-control, it naturally informs all aspects of our lives. It influences the way we engage in conflict and conversations, guides our food and drinking habits and choices, informs our sexual life, and helps us express our emotions in healthy ways. Essentially, self-control is about being masters of our physical, cognitive, and emotional functions, and knowing how to regulate and keep them in alignment with our souls' desires. A great deal of this regulation comes naturally when we align with the essence of our soul, but we can supplement it by actively utilizing tools and practices. For example, spiritual practices like meditation and energy healing; cognitive practices, such as journaling, EFT tapping, and psychotherapy; and somatic practices, such as yoga and flexibility training, are all ways of regulating ourselves through the virtue of self-control.

A great formula for practicing self-control is starting with self-awareness, which leads to self-respect, which eventually results in self-control. When we take the time to become aware of our authentic nature through inner work and our spiritual practice, we also become aware of our authentic values, needs, and desires—those that are in alignment with our life purpose and highest potential. Once we know these, we practice self-respect by actualizing them and avoiding activities that oppose them. Consequently, we practice self-control.

As a personal example, I know that once I have more than two drinks when I'm out, I go on a downward spiral. I'll soon light up a cigarette or two, get bombarded by self-defeating thoughts, and start saying and doing things I know I will regret later. I've done enough inner work to know this about myself, and to also know what my values are. Consequently, I actively choose to respect myself by practicing self-control when I go out. If I didn't have that self-awareness, I wouldn't be able to do so, and I'd get myself into trouble every time I went out.

It's important to note that the Greek virtue of self-control is not to be confused with the Christian rendition of it, which is more about self-restriction. When Christianity talks about self-control, it's usually associated with restricting physical pleasures, since it perceives the physical body as something sinful, and something we're meant to supersede rather than enjoy. According to (my understanding of) Christian thought, the body is the enemy and only the soul matters. This is a key distinction from Greek thought, which not only accepts, but also respects, honors, and actively enjoys the body and its pleasures. The virtue of self-control from the Greek perspective isn't about denying the body, but about knowing and respecting its limits.

Ascending with Artemis

The practices in this section will help you align with Artemis's qualities and embody her essence.

Activation Mantra

I embrace my pure, raw, and wild nature.

Taking a moment to center and ground yourself, place both hands on your heart or extend your arms up to the sky, and repeat this affirmation a few times or for as long as it takes to feel its essence. Rather than just saying the words, focus on embodying each word and truly understanding the meaning of what you're saying. Employ all your senses so that you can see, feel, hear, smell, and taste the qualities of the mantra.

Ascension Journal Prompts

Take out your journal and let yourself free-write your answers to these questions. These are meant to help you explore Artemis's primary qualities in your life, creating opportunities for healing and growth:

- What comes to mind when you think of pure, raw, wild energy?
- Who are you without your ego?
- What lessons have you learned in your life's transitions?
- What does it mean to take action by consulting both your head and your heart?
- How can you respect your body, mind, and spirit more?

Connecting with Artemis Out in Nature

The best place to experience Artemis is in forests and mountains untouched and undamaged by humans. Depending on where you live, locate a park or forest that's as unspoiled by humans as possible, and go for a walk there alone or with a friend (provided that it's safe for you to do so).

Before you start your walk, set the intention to connect with Artemis's pure, raw, and wild Divine Feminine energy. Take a few moments to close your eyes, center and ground yourself, and awaken your five senses. Then, open your eyes and take an intuitively guided, mindful walk in the wilderness. While walking, be hyperaware of your senses—what you see, hear, feel, smell, taste, and know. Pay attention to how your body responds to your surrounding environment, and what you feel guided to do. Trust your impulses and let Artemis guide the way.

The aim of this practice is to entrain yourself with the purity and wildness of nature, so you can awaken your own pure and wild feminine energy. As noted earlier in the book, *entrainment* means aligning your vibrational frequency with the vibrational frequency of something else—in this case, nature. All natural environments, and especially wild, untouched natural spaces, have a poignantly high vibrational frequency that dominates the area. By simply inserting ourselves into natural spaces, we allow our energies to merge and tune in to the dominant frequency. On this occasion, you'll be tuning in to the frequency of Artemis.

At the end of your walk, have a chat with your friend or journal about your experience. This is a great time to use the journal prompts from the previous section and receive divine guidance from Artemis.

Orphic Hymn to Artemis

Use this ancient Artemis hymn whenever you need to deeply activate or call upon Artemis's presence. Ideally, stand straight, extend your hands up to the sky, and recite the hymn out loud.

> *Hear me, O queen,*
> *Zeus's daughter of many names,*
> *Titanic and Bacchic,*
> *revered, renowned archer,*
> *torch-bearing goddess bringing light to all,*
> *Diktynna, helper at childbirth,*
> *you help women in labor,*
> *though you know not what labor is.*

O frenzy-loving huntress,
you loosen girdles and drive distress away;
swift arrow-pouring goddess of the outdoors,
you roam in the night.
Fame-bringing and affable,
redeeming and masculine in appearance,
Orthia, goddess of swift birth,
you are a nurturer of mortal youths,
immortal and yet of this earth,
you slay wild beasts, O blessed one,
your realm is in the mountain forest,
you hunt deer.
O revered and mighty queen of all,
fair-blossomed, eternal,
sylvan, dog-loving,
many-shaped lady of Kydonia,
come, dear goddess,
as savior to all the initiates,
accessible to all, bringing forth
the beautiful fruit of the earth,
lovely peace,
and fair-tressed health.
May you dispatch diseases and pain
to the peaks of the mountains.

Artemis's Symbolism

As you feel guided, use the following to invite Artemis's essence into your home and sacred spaces. You can also use these symbols to set up an Artemis altar, as explained in Chapter 23.

- **Colors:** Silver, brown, green, amethyst, white, crocus
- **Symbols:** Torch, bow, arrow
- **Sacred animals:** Wolf, deer, bear, cat, boar, goat, wild dog

- **Sacred plants/fruits:** Wormwood, amaranth, palm, cypress tree, peanut
- **Offerings:** Cedar, jasmine, myrtle, white flowers, frankincense incense, tokens of deer

Activation Meditation

Sit in a relaxed position, close your eyes, get into a meditative state using the Meditation Prep Process, and follow these steps to activate Artemis's energy within you:

1. Having relaxed your body, continue by relaxing your mind, clearing it of incoming thoughts. As thoughts come in, visualize them as energetic bubbles that float out of your head and disappear in the ether. To clear your mind further, find something small to focus on, such as the beating of your heart, the whistling of the wind, or the ticking of the clock. By giving your mind a rhythmic pattern to focus on, you satisfy its urge to think while preventing upsetting or anxious thoughts from coming in.

2. Once your body and mind are both deeply relaxed, call upon Artemis's essence by affirming "I am Artemis" mentally or aloud. Using the "I am" affirmation is a powerful mantra for embodying the goddess's energy. While repeating this affirmation, you'll eventually feel Artemis's presence. You may see her with your mind's eye, feel her strength, or notice her through your other senses. Take a moment to acknowledge and welcome her.

   She shows up as a young huntress with a short skirt, hunting boots, silver arrows on her back, and a stag by her side. Her aura radiates a smooth silver light that releases any remaining tension from your body and connects you to the purity of your soul.

3. Artemis invites you to go on a journey of raising your vibration and aligning yourself with the frequency of your highest self. Taking you by the hands, she pulls your astral body out of your physical body so you can travel together across the dimensions. With a jump, you both leap off the ground and fly together over the Earth, moving through its auric layers. This upward journey through the Earth's aura both cleanses your energy

and raises your vibration, as you can enter the higher planes of existence only if your energy is clear and your vibration high.

4. As you fly higher and higher with Artemis and her stag by your side, you feel fears, frustrations, and limiting beliefs shed from your energy. Any concerns you've had about yourself, your purpose, other people, and the world melt away, and you gradually gain a higher perspective. As a result, your vibration rises higher and higher, and you're able to enter the second and third planes of existence.

5. The third plane of existence at the outskirts of the Earth's aura, the spiritual plane, is Artemis's training ground for mature souls. She guides you to come to a halt and acclimatize with the energy of this plane. As you look around, you see your personal spirit guides, minor gods and goddesses, daimons and heroes, and other high-vibrational entities that inhabit this realm. Spend some time exploring and letting your energy align with the frequency of this realm. Feel free to chat with your spirit guides and other loving guides in that realm, receiving guidance that'll help you follow your purpose and ascension journey.

6. Having cleansed your energy of fears and limiting beliefs, and raised your vibration to match the frequency of the spiritual plane, Artemis can now gift you with her purity. Taking an etheric silver arrow from her quiver, she points her bow at your heart, ready to shoot. Willingly, you stand straight facing her, ready to receive this activation. As she shoots the arrow, it enters your etheric heart and fills it with a silvery light that expands all through your body and aura, purifying and raising your vibration further. This light works on a deep level within your energetic field to guide and speed up your soul's journey of ascension. Take some time to breathe deeply and let your body adjust to this shift.

7. Once you feel settled in your new energetic state, it's time to return to your body. Artemis invites you to fly together down the Earth's layers and back to your physical body. As you fall back into your body, you have a renewed sense of yourself, your purpose, your soul's journey, and the world as a

whole. You appreciate this higher perspective and set an intention to let it inspire your life moving forward.

8. When the process feels complete, thank Artemis for this energetic upgrade and gently wake up your body with small, slow movements. If you wish, take out your journal and use the journal prompts to channel more specific guidance, or make notes of the guidance you received during the meditation.

You can download an extended guided recording of this meditation at *www.GeorgeLizos.com/SOGM.*

CHAPTER 20

Hestia

I t wouldn't be an understatement to say that, from a mythological standpoint, Hestia is the most boring of the Greek gods. While the other Olympians fought the Giants, obsessed over mortals, and plotted against each other, Hestia remained at Olympus, faithfully guarding the sacred home fires. In Athens, there was even disagreement as to whether Hestia or Dionysus were to be included in the list of the 12 gods: the east frieze of the Parthenon depicted Dionysus as one of the Olympians, whereas the gods' altar at the Agora included Hestia instead.

Furthermore, very few temples were dedicated to Hestia in ancient times, and in the rare depictions we have of her, she was portrayed as a modestly cloaked woman in a head veil. And yet, despite her blasé appearance, mythology, and characteristics, one could argue that Hestia was the most venerated of all Greek gods and goddesses. As the goddess of the hearth, Hestia had an altar in every household, temple, and city-state, and she received the first offering and libation in most religious ceremonies.

When I first started my household practice to the gods and set up my altar, the first statue I put up, and the one that remains there throughout the year no matter the gods I'm working with, is Hestia's. Every morning, I go to my altar, light Hestia's hearth (a candle), extend my hands up to the sky, and recite her Orphic hymn (it's the only one I've memorized). Hestia's hearth stands for the heart of the house, but also the physical and spiritual hearts of my body and soul. As I light the candle, I feel my house's energy come alive and my heart chakra opening up, and I'm overtaken by a deep sense of calm, security, and connectedness to my home, myself, others, and the entire world.

Lighting Hestia's hearth is a sacred act that reminds me of everything that is home—my actual house, my body, my neighborhood, my city, the world, the cosmos, the entire Universe. Beyond physical spaces, I'm reminded of my virtual homes—my Instagram account, Facebook group, website, YouTube channel, and two podcasts. I also think of the sense of home I feel while I'm with my family, friends, and peers. Finally, I'm reminded of my past lives' various homes on this planet and beyond, as well as my home in the spirit world.

When we feel lost, alone, and disconnected from ourselves and purpose—when we've strayed away from home—Hestia is there with her fiery torch, lighting the path and guiding our way back home. To ourselves, to others, and to the gods.

The Essence of Hestia

Hestia's the goddess of the domestic, civic, and spiritual hearth (her name means hearth); family; the home; and the state. Like Hephaestus, she represents fire. While they both channel the same primal fire of creation, Hephaestus expresses the masculine side of fire and Hestia its feminine qualities. Hephaestus's expression of fire is concerned with the creation of human beings and the physical and spiritual tools we need to thrive in our life, purpose, and ascension journeys. Thus, Hephaestus's fire is more extroverted. He creates and transforms in a more practical and outwardly way, turning thoughts to things. Conversely, Hestia's fire is concerned with the creation of our homes and communities. Her fire creates safe, warm, and nurturing homes and communities, and strengthens the bonds between the people within them. As a rule of thumb, Hestia helps us nurture our creative potential, and Hephaestus helps us express it.

When we think of Hestia, we usually relate her to our homes, but for many people home is more than just their household. Hence, Hestia is at the center of all kinds of communities that share a space and provide a home for people. These could be physical spaces shared with family, friends, roommates, colleagues, neighborhoods, cities, counties, and the entire world. They could also be virtual communities (such as Facebook groups, forums, and online memberships) or even spiritual communities sharing energetic space (such as the space we share with our soul families, spirit guides, and our guardian gods and goddesses). Whatever the space and the community, Hestia's hearth is at the center, magnetizing everyone together, strengthening and growing the relationships.

Consequently, Hestia is the protector of our various homes and communities. Her fire helps nurture a sense of security within the community, provides a safe platform from which people can grow together, and generates prosperity for the members. For this reason, Hestia was an omnipresent goddess during the ancient times. Every single household and city-state had a central hearth dedicated to the goddess constantly lit, and during religious ceremonies people would lay their offerings and libations to her first before any other god. The communal hearth at Delphi was often seen as the hearth for the whole of Greece. So important was Hestia's presence within communities that both the household and city members had a sacred duty to keep the hearth lit at all times; the hearth would die out only if the whole family had passed away or the city or state had fallen.

On a spiritual level, Hestia's hearth is at the core of all creation. Our body is our soul's home, and our heart is our soul's hearth. Furthermore, the nucleus within each cell of our body is that cell's hearth, and this is the case for all animate beings and inanimate objects in the cosmos. From this perspective, every bit of consciousness in the cosmos has a piece of Hestia's sacred fire within them, serving as the powerhouse of life-force energy that keeps things moving and growing. The ancients understood Hestia's ubiquitous nature and central importance in creation and dedicated a hearth to her within every god's temple, which also explains why Hestia didn't have many temples in ancient times.

In Greece, Hestia's sacred hearth was often seen as a conscious being, so much so that the hearth was often used instead of a statue to signify Hestia's presence. Similarly, during the ceremonies we perform at the Modern Temple of Zeus in Cyprus, we don't use Hestia's statue but rather a central hearth on a tripod that represents Hestia during the ceremony. Both in ancient and modern times, the hearth serves the purpose of feeding people, warming up the space, and being a central meeting point for bonding and socialization between the family and community members. Spiritually, the hearth stands for people's hearts, and its ever-present energy helps us access our emotions, align with our souls' calling, and keep connected with our hearts' desires and purpose.

On a soul level, Hestia's hearth is also the core of our human souls and guides our ascension journeys. Hestia's the divine intelligence within our souls, taking guidance from the gods, coming up with our soul purposes, and choosing our future incarnations. Evolving spiritually is about aligning our bodies' and souls' hearths so they can effectively communicate and guide our journeys forward.

Hestia's Virtues

Hestia's two main virtues that you can embody to follow your purpose and path to spiritual ascension are stability and decency.

Stability

In the same way that Hestia is omnipresent in all creation, so, too, is her virtue of stability, or *statherotita* in Greek. Stability is a central characteristic of all the gods, functions, and laws of the Universe, presided over by Hestia. Thus, beyond just being a human virtue that we can practice, it's also the true state of things. Stability affirms that the divine systems and laws that run the Universe are robust and perfect; therefore, everything that happens does so within the realm of Universal laws. From this perspective, nothing ever really goes wrong and all is always well. Knowing and accepting this truth immediately gives us a higher perspective on both our personal lives and global matters, which helps us create stability within and without.

Practicing the virtue of stability primarily involves becoming aware of and consistently practicing our personal core values. The *Oxford Learners Dictionary* defines values as "beliefs about what is right and wrong and what is important in life." Therefore, our personal core values serve as standards or guidelines about our beliefs, behaviors, and the choices we make in life. To discover your core values, you can start by asking yourself questions such as, "What makes me happy?" and "What's important to me?" Notice what comes up. Examples of core values include honesty, dependability, and generosity. As you continue doing the inner work, deepening your spiritual journey, and aligning with your soul's essence, your core values will come up naturally.

One of the most important aspects of the virtue of stability is consistency. Our core values often draw from, and are intrinsically tied with, our life purpose and the specific desires aligned to it. Thus, practicing stability is about taking focused and deliberate action toward our goals and life purpose. Rather than self-sabotage with distractions and unimportant tasks, or being dissuaded by people's opinions about our work, stability asks us to stick to our goals until we've fulfilled them. In the words of Stoic philosopher Epictetus, "To live a life of virtue, you have to become consistent, even when it isn't convenient, comfortable, or easy."[1]

Stability presupposes that we understand our duty in the world and the Universe. *Duty* is an umbrella term that includes living by Universal laws, following the commonly agreed rules and regulations of society, consciously pursuing our four purposes (as explained in Chapter 5), and respecting other people's journeys and purposes, too. Although *duty* is a loaded term that tends to have a negative connotation of struggling to be someone and do something we don't want to, it's really a process of surrendering and aligning with our authentic nature, which is already in alignment with the aforementioned purposes.

Decency

The virtue of decency, or *kosmiotis* in Greek, directly translates to "be like the cosmos." Thus, to understand and practice this virtue, we need to first understand the true essence of the cosmos. As I shared in Chapter 2, "In Greek the word *cosmos* means jewel and adornment, as the cosmos is the part of the Universe that has acquired natural order and has attained harmony and beauty. . . . The cosmos maintains the Universe's qualities of being absolute, infinite, and unchangeable." From this perspective, practicing decency has to do with bringing the cosmos's inner and outer beauty, and natural order, to a human level.

Our personal cosmos is our inner self and physical body; therefore, an aspect of practicing decency has to do with self-care. The ancient Greeks placed equal emphasis on developing inner and outer beauty. They cultivated inner beauty through deep thinking, learning, and embodying the gods' virtues, and they invested in their outer beauty through exercise, good food, and a healthy lifestyle. The sculptures of the gods and goddesses were meant to epitomize the Greek beauty standards, so gods are almost always portrayed looking fit and healthy, with perfectly symmetrical bodies, and exuding the essence of their main virtues and qualities.

To embody the beauty and orderliness of the cosmos, we also need to respect and actively add to it. From an external point of view, this means taking care of our homes, cities, and the planet. Our homes reflect our inner world, and vice versa. Thus, by consciously clearing and ordering our living space, we also clear and order our inner world. Similarly, when we actively clean, protect, and respect our neighborhoods and cities, nature, and the world at large, we add to the beauty and orderliness of the world, which always reflects our inner state, too. Being kind to others is another easy practice we can use to add to the world's, and our own, inner beauty. Simple acts of kindness, such as being a good listener, giving compliments, and opening the door for someone, affirm and amplify the orderliness of the world and help us nurture it within, too.

The Universe doesn't settle for mediocrity, and you shouldn't either. Imagine if the laws of the Universe didn't always work as expected. One day the sun rises; the next day it doesn't. Today gravity works perfectly; tomorrow we're all falling upward. It wouldn't inspire confidence in the gods or the Universe, would it? Thankfully, the gods have high standards for how they run the Universe, and we can count on them. The question is: Do you have equally high standards for yourself? To truly mirror the orderliness of the cosmos and practice decency, we have to set high standards for ourselves and reach our potential. This isn't about reaching for unrealistic standards of perfection, but rather knowing who we are and what we can do, and going for it.

Unfortunately, we live in a society that nurtures mediocrity and complacency. Instead of being encouraged to explore our talents, follow our dreams, and reach our potential, we're conditioned to repress our gifts, play it safe, and become cogs in other people's dreams. Practicing decency is about becoming aware of our conditioning and having the courage to dream bigger. As Seneca wrote in his 25th letter to Lucilius, "You are engaged in making of yourself the sort of person in whose company you would not dare to sin. . . . You ought to make yourself of a different stamp from the multitude."[2]

Ascending with Hestia

The practices in this section will help you align with Hestia's qualities and embody her essence.

Activation Mantra

I am home.

Taking a moment to center and ground yourself, place both hands on your heart or extend your arms up to the sky, and repeat this affirmation a few times or for as long as it takes to feel its essence. Rather than just saying the words, focus on embodying each word and truly understanding the meaning of what you're saying. Employ all your senses so that you can see, feel, hear, smell, and taste the qualities of the mantra.

Ascension Journal Prompts

Take out your journal and let yourself free-write your answers to these questions. These are meant to help you explore Hestia's primary qualities in your life, creating opportunities for healing and growth:

- What's home for you?
- How can you further strengthen your closest relationships?
- Make a list of your personal core values. How can you practice them more consistently?
- How can you bring more beauty and order into your house?
- In what areas of your life have you settled for mediocrity?

Connecting with Hestia Out in Nature

Because she is a goddess of the house, the best place to connect with Hestia is in the nature of your home. The physical and energetic states of our homes mirror our own physical and energetic states. For example, a cluttered house is usually a sign of a cluttered mind, and an energetically stained house will most likely create energetic stains within your own aura, too. Therefore, by consciously decluttering, cleansing, and taking care of your home, you create changes within you, too.

Here are three ways you can take better care of your home with Hestia's help:

- **Candle space clearing:** An easy way to clear the energy of your house is by working with fire. Light a candle with the intention of burning negative or stagnant energy in the house and then walk around your house with it, visualizing its glow expanding through the space and cleansing it. Ask Hestia to walk with you and channel the firelight into the corners and spaces of the house that most need it.
- **Decluttering:** Simply put, things you don't use create stagnant energy that lower the vibration of your house, and therefore, of yourself. While there

are many decluttering systems you can use (I recommend Marie Kondo's method), you can start the process by donating, gifting, or throwing away five things you haven't used in the past year every week for a month. This one-month challenge will get you feeling comfortable with decluttering, so you can eventually take a more thorough approach.

● **Meet the spirit of your house:** Your house, like everything in the Universe, has spirit and consciousness, too. In meditation, ask Hestia to introduce you to the spirit of your home. Start by becoming conscious of your house's rooms and their energies, and call upon its spirit to make herself present. Your house's spirit may show up in whatever form makes sense for you. When it does, ask for her name as well as for guidance in taking better care of her.

Orphic Hymn to Hestia

Use this ancient Hestia hymn whenever you need to deeply activate or call upon Hestia's presence. Ideally, stand straight, extend your hands up to the sky, and recite the hymn out loud.

> *Queen Hestia,*
> *daughter of mighty Kronos,*
> *mistress of ever-burning fire,*
> *you dwell in the center of the house.*
> *May you raise the holy initiates*
> *in these sacred rites,*
> *may you grant them unwithering youth,*
> *wealth as well, prudence and purity.*
> *Home of the blessed gods,*
> *men's mighty buttress,*
> *eternal, many-shaped,*
> *beloved, grass-yellow,*
> *smile, O blessed one,*
> *kindly accept these offerings,*
> *waft upon us prosperity,*
> *breathe upon us gentle-handed health.*

Hestia's Symbolism

As you feel guided, use the following to invite Hestia's essence into your home and sacred spaces. You can also use these symbols to set up a Hestia altar, as explained in Chapter 23.

- **Color:** White
- **Symbols:** Hearth, veil, altar, ring of fire
- **Sacred animal:** Pig
- **Offerings:** Various fragrances of incense

Activation Meditation

Sit in a relaxed position, close your eyes, get into a meditative state using the Meditation Prep Process, and follow these steps to activate Hestia's energy within you:

1. Bring your attention to your heart chakra in the center of your chest. As you psychically look inside your heart chakra, you'll notice a tiny flame emerging. Breathe deeply, and with each breath you take, visualize this flame starting to grow bigger and brighter. Keep going until the flame has grown big enough to fill up your entire heart chakra. This fire is your soul's healing, creative, and recalibrating life-force energy.

2. Once your heart's hearth is lit, call upon Hestia's essence by affirming "I am Hestia" mentally or aloud. Using the "I am" affirmation is a powerful mantra for embodying the goddess's energy. While repeating this affirmation, you'll eventually feel Hestia's presence. You may see her with your mind's eye, feel her strength, or notice her through your other senses. Take a moment to acknowledge and welcome her.

   She shows up as a modest-cloaked woman wearing a white veil and holding a lighted torch. She radiates a pure white light that calms your nerves and makes you feel at ease and at home.

3. Hestia extends her torch of sacred fire toward your heart, blessing and activating your inner fire. As soon as she does so, the fire within your heart gradually starts to expand throughout your body. It first seeps through your vital organs, cleansing them of toxic or stagnant energy, revitalizing them,

and restoring them to a state of homeostasis. The fire expands through the core of your body, your head, arms, and legs, until your entire body is saturated with this healing frequency.

4. Then, Hestia guides this healing fire to extend outside of your body and into your auric field. Breathe deeply as the fire seeps through all seven layers of your aura, letting it cleanse your energetic field and strengthen your energetic defences.

5. As Hestia's fire within and around you keeps growing larger and stronger, it now reaches out of your energetic field to fill the space you're in, followed by your house, your neighborhood, city, country, continent, the entire world, and the Universe. Let this process unfold naturally, and feel your energetic field expand to encompass these spaces, claiming them as your home.

6. Having let your inner fire envelop the entire Universe, mentally direct this fire to reach the people and communities you're part of, including virtual ones. Set the intention that the fire clears any blocks that hinder these relationships and also strengthens the bonds between you so that you get to support each other and grow together.

7. Finally, when the process feels complete, bring your attention back to your heart and visualize your heart as a magnet, drawing the fire in and shrinking your energetic field. Let the fire grow smaller until it reaches the boundaries of your heart chakra.

8. To end the meditation, thank Hestia for this energetic upgrade and gently wake up your body with small, slow movements. If you wish, take out your journal and use the journal prompts to channel more specific guidance, or make notes of the guidance you received during the meditation.

You can download an extended guided recording of this meditation at *www.GeorgeLizos.com/SOGM.*

CHAPTER 21

Meet Your Guardian God or Goddess

Having met the 12 gods and goddesses, you're now ready to meet your guardian god or goddess. Before we incarnate on the planet, we're all assigned a god or goddess to guide us along our journey. This god is chosen based on a few factors, including our specific life and soul purposes, the stage we're in on our ascension path, as well as our soul and human dispositions.

Our guardian god or goddess accompanies us throughout our lives (and often in future lives, too), and they act as our main points of contact when communicating with the other gods and goddesses and the spirit world at large. Throughout our lives, we can have additional guardian gods and goddesses that work with us, depending on the stage we're in and the current lessons we're working on. For example, my guardian god is Apollo, who guides my blend of life purpose, including my spiritual, acting, and singing careers. For many years, however, I was assigned Aphrodite as a guardian goddess to help me heal sexual trauma and nurture self-love.

Your guardian god or goddess may or may not be one of the 12 Olympians. Remember, there are as many gods and goddesses as there are Universal laws and functions. Therefore, your guardian god or goddess may be a secondary god, such as Asclepius, Dionysus, Pan, Eros, Hecate, one of the muses, or any one of the other minor gods. During the meditation that follows, keep yourself open to connecting with your guardian god or goddess without having expectations as to who that may be.

Meditation for Meeting Your Guardian God or Goddess

Sit in a relaxed position, close your eyes, get into a meditative state using the Meditation Prep Process, and follow these steps to meet your guardian god or goddess:

1. Visualize yourself stepping into a beautiful garden. It's the most beautiful garden you've ever seen. Let yourself experience this garden with all your senses. Feel the wet grass beneath your feet, stare up at the sun and feel its warmth on your body, feel the gentle breeze caressing your face, and smell the fragrant, colorful flowers all around you. This is a garden of your soul, a safe space for you to spend time with yourself and your spirit guides.

2. As you get accustomed to the garden, mentally ask the 12 Olympians and secondary and minor gods and goddesses to join you. They enter the garden and stand in a circle around you, beaming their divine light in every direction. Take a moment to bathe in their collective frequencies that raise your vibration.

3. When you feel ready, ask your guardian god or goddess to step forth and make themselves known. Let go of your expectations and allow this process to take place naturally. As the god or goddess steps forward, notice who they are and take a bow of gratitude. If you don't recognize the god, ask them who they are and pay attention to the way they look so you can research them later.

4. Take as much time as you want to communicate with your guardian god or goddess. Ask them why they chose to work with you in this life, any questions you have about your life or soul purposes, and any guidance they have for you moving forward.

5. Once you feel complete, thank your guardian god or goddess for being with you and guiding you in this life, and ask them to stay close and support you moving forward. Gently wake up your body with small, slow movements and come out of the meditation, feeling great! If you wish, take out your journal and make notes of the guidance you received during the meditation.

You can download an extended guided recording of this meditation at *www.GeorgeLizos.com/SOGM.*

PART III

Connecting
with the
Gods

CHAPTER 22

A Year with the Gods

There are many ways to work with the Greek gods and goddesses, both as part of your spiritual practice as well as in your day-to-day activities. In this part of the book, I'll share a few that are modeled after ancient practices and rituals, as well as the practices I've personally used to strengthen my relationship with the gods as part of following my life purpose and ascension journey. These exercises will range from setting up altars to performing rituals and practicing manifestation exercises. In Appendices 1 and 2, I share additional guidance on developing your intuition to receive clear signs and communication from the gods and goddesses.

In this chapter, we'll discuss the various festivals and rituals you can perform on a monthly basis to celebrate and connect with the gods and goddesses, as well as to manifest your purpose and desires in a systematic way.

The Greek Wheel of the Year

If you're a practicing pagan or participate in other Earth-based spiritual practices, you're probably familiar with the Wheel of the Year. This is an annual cycle of seasonal festivals centered around solar events and their midpoints. Historical evidence suggests that the Wheel of the Year as we know it today is a combination of Celtic and Anglo-Saxon festivals. It usually consists of the following festivals: winter solstice

(20–23 December), Imbolc (1 February), spring equinox (19–22 March), Beltane (1 May), summer solstice (19–23 June), Lammas (1 August), autumn equinox (21–24 September), and Samhain (1 November). In the Southern Hemisphere, these dates are usually advanced six months to coincide with their seasons.

Since ancient Greece was divided into different city-states rather than being a unified country, each city-state had its own festival calendar celebrating its patron gods and other holidays. Although many of the calendars' festivals correlated with lunar and seasonal events, there wasn't a common festival calendar for the whole of Greece.

Consequently, the Supreme Council of Ethnic Hellenes (YSEE) created a contemporary Greek Wheel of the Year to guide religious practices. Rather than a reconstruction of the ancient tradition, this new calendar is an evolution of the ancient practices for the modern pagan. Centered around the cycle of the sun to correspond with the Celtic Wheel of the Year, each month features a god or goddess, an ancient festival, the month's zodiac sign, and the virtues of the venerated god. Although each month features a single god or goddess, they're also accompanied by their divine couple for the purpose of balancing the masculine and feminine energies.

Starting in January and ending in December, the Greek Wheel of the Year also provides a guided framework for aligning our manifestation efforts, life purpose, and spiritual journeys to the cyclic nature of the Earth.

Month	Sun sign	Gods	Virtues	Festival
January	Aquarius	Hera with Zeus	Fearless speech, pride	Theogamia
February	Pisces	Poseidon with Demeter	Piety, goodness	Anthesteria
March	Aries	Athena with Hephaestus	Fortitude, quickness of mind	Asclepieia/Spring equinox
April	Taurus	Aphrodite with Ares	Friendship, generosity	Charisia/Aphrodisia
May	Gemini	Apollo with Artemis	Harmony, sincerity	Thargelia

Month	Sun sign	Gods	Virtues	Festival
June	Cancer	Hermes with Hestia	Fair dealing, sociability	Summer solstice
July	Leo	Zeus with Hera	Justice, orderliness	Dioskouria
August	Virgo	Demeter with Poseidon	Endurance, prudence	Heraia
September	Libra	Hephaestus with Athena	Industriousness, resourcefulness	Autumn equinox
October	Scorpio	Ares with Aphrodite	Bravery, courage	Heracleia
November	Sagittarius	Artemis with Apollo	Temperance, self-control	Maimakteria
December	Capricorn	Hestia with Hermes	Stability, decency	Winter solstice/ Triesperon

Here's a summary of the 12 festivals and what each celebrates:

Theogamia translates to "sacred marriage" and celebrates the divine union between the king and queen of Olympus, Zeus and Hera. Their wedding symbolizes the union of the Divine Masculine and Feminine energies, the two primal energies that create the cosmos. Similarly, during this time we also make a sacred promise to ourselves by setting and committing to intentions and resolutions for the new year. The Theogamia also marks the start of a new cycle in our spiritual ascension journey, through which we'll grow, learn lessons, and expand our consciousness.

In ancient times, the **Anthesteria** festival celebrated the beginning of spring and was a three-day celebration that included the opening of new wine, wine-drinking contests, the celebration of the sacred wedding between Dionysus and the city, and paying respects to the ancestors. Due to the communion with the world of the dead, the festival is marked by feelings of excitement and joy, as well as sadness and mystery. Dionysus, who moves through contradiction on all cosmic levels, is characterized by this duality. He is both visible and invisible, dead and alive, wild and civilized.

Consequently, during the Anthesteria festival we celebrate the cyclic nature of life, and Dionysus's contribution to the rebirth of nature and of ourselves. Paying respect to the ancestors is a way of recognizing the cyclic nature of life and appreciating our ancestors' contribution to the evolution of human consciousness. The ruling god of the month is Poseidon, who also has a connection with change, transformation, and the underworld. During this month, we leverage the cyclic and transformative energies of nature to kickstart our path on manifesting our desires, following our purpose, and expanding our consciousness.

The **Asclepieia or spring equinox** festival, on March 20–23 in the Northern Hemisphere and September 20–23 in the Southern Hemisphere, marks the beginning of spring, from which point the days start growing longer than the nights, resulting in physical and spiritual renewal. The increased sunlight restores our energy field, amplifies our creativity, and boosts our drive for following our desires and purpose. Aside from Athena, during this time we also honor the god of medicine, Asclepius, who progressively imparts on us the main energetic qualities of the physical and spiritual sun, as an energy clearer, healer, and saviour, until the summer solstice.

The **Charisia/Aphrodisia** festival celebrates the completed rebirth of nature through Aphrodite's regenerating power. The festival is also dedicated to the Three Graces, or *Charites* in Greek—Aglaea (Shining), Euphrosyne (Joy), and Thalia (Blooming)—Aphrodite's consorts and nature goddesses who express Aphrodite's qualities in the world. Spiritually, this is a time during which our bodies and souls have fully awakened following the winter months and increased solar energy, and we're making increasing progress in following our purpose and manifesting our desires.

The **Thargelia** festival is named after the first harvest and celebrates the richness and fertility of the Earth following its regeneration by Aphrodite. This festival is marked by the birth of the twin gods, Apollo and Artemis, whose combined qualities nourish the soil, protect from pollution, and bring about an abundant harvest. Similarly, this is a time for us to start reaping the fruits of our labor from all the work we've been putting in. In the same way that Apollo's divine light fertilizes and matures the crops, it also fertilizes and matures our desires and purpose, leading to their manifestation. Spiritually, Apollo's increasing light and Artemis's purity during this month help us awaken our own inner light and purity, leading to powerful epiphanies that speed up our ascension journey.

The **summer solstice**, on June 20–21 in the Northern Hemisphere and December 21–22 in the Southern Hemisphere, marks the longest day of the year and the beginning of summer. On this day, we celebrate Apollo, whose light and presence are now at their peak; the sun god, Helios; and the ruling god of the month, Hermes. During this time, flowers are in full bloom, trees are bountiful with fruits, and nature is at its most expressive stage. Similarly, our manifestation power is at its maximum, and we usually get to enjoy greater abundance and fulfillment as more and more desires are coming to fruition. Concurrently, the energy of the summer solstice upgrades our energetic blueprint and speeds up our progress on our purpose and ascension journey.

The **Dioskouria** festival honors Zeus's twin sons, Castor and Polydeuces (or Pollux). According to the myth, when Castor (who was mortal) was killed, his immortal brother Pollux asked Zeus to resurrect him. To align with Universal laws, Pollux offered to share his time in the underworld with Castor so that they could alternate between the living and the dead. Touched by their brotherly love, Zeus transformed them into stars that now form part of the Gemini constellation.

Consequently, the Dioskouria festival is another reminder to honor the cyclic nature of life and our souls. Castor and Pollux help us see the bigger picture and gain a deeper perspective on life and our spiritual paths. By acknowledging the immortality of our souls, we realize that our journey never truly ends, which takes the pressure off and allows us to better flow with and enjoy life.

The **Heraia** were a female festival and sporting games held every four years at Olympia, probably around the same time as the Olympic Games. Whereas the Olympic Games were dedicated to Zeus, the Heraia were dedicated to Hera and celebrated her feminine qualities. The worship of female goddesses at Olympia is very ancient and was connected to the fertility of the Earth and the resulting prosperity it brought to the community. Therefore, this festival is also connected with the Earth goddess, Demeter, and the fruitfulness of the crops, the earth, and ourselves during this time of the year.

According to scholars, the female winner of the Heraia games would marry the male winner of the Olympic Games, signifying the completed cycle of land cultivation brought forth by Hera's and Zeus's primordial feminine and masculine energies.

The **autumn equinox**, on September 20–23 in the Northern Hemisphere and March 20–23 in the Southern Hemisphere, marks the beginning of autumn, from which point the nights start growing longer than the days. This is signified by goddess Persephone's descent to the underworld, and therefore the gradual withering of the Earth as we move towards the winter solstice. As the days get shorter, we also use more artificial light and heating, which is one of the reasons this month's ruling god is Hephaestus.

Whereas the spring equinox is marked by increased energy and action-taking, the autumn equinox's energy is all about recession, relaxation, and looking within. This is a time of appreciating and celebrating the abundance of the Earth, reaping the benefits of our labor, and preparing for change.

The **Heracleia** festival honors Heracles (or Hercules), the sun god that rules over the darker, wintery months of the year. As a result of the waning solar power, the Earth shifts attention from expression and extroversion toward recalibration and introversion, as it withers, gathers its energy, and prepares the soil for its resurrection in the following spring equinox. Similarly, during this time Hercules guides us to shift our attention from creation to self-introspection, so we can assess our journey thus far and prepare the energy for what's to come. The ruling god of the month is Ares, whose virtues of bravery and courage equip us with embracing this energetic shift and the benefits it brings.

The **Maimakteria** festival is in honor of Zeus Maimaktes, meaning blusterous. Zeus Maimaktes is the aspect of Zeus that symbolizes the unpredictable weather conditions at the beginning of the winter months. In ancient times, this festival was a way of appeasing the god and praying for a mild but rainy winter, which would eventually lead to fertile land and abundant crops. As a result, apart from Zeus, during this time we also celebrate the raw, wild, and unbridled energy of

Artemis, as well as other nature deities, such as the Nymphs and the Hours. This month is a great time to reconnect with the purity of your soul, refine your purpose's definition, assess your desires, and start thinking about what you wish to accomplish in the new year.

The **winter solstice or Triesperon**, on December 20–23 in the Northern Hemisphere and June 20–23 in the Southern Hemisphere, marks the shortest day of the year and the beginning of winter. During these three days, the length of the day and night is the same, and on the night of the 24th through the 25th, the days start growing longer again. *Triesperon* translates to "three nights" in Greek, signifying this natural phenomenon. As a result, during this time we celebrate the birth of the sun, symbolized by the birth of baby Hercules or Dionysus, depending on the tradition.

The winter solstice represents a time of planting the first seeds, intentions, and desires; the return of the sun; and the promise that things will start to grow again. Spiritually, the birth of the sun in December leading into Theogamia in January signifies the beginning of a new spiritual journey, with new lessons to learn, challenges to overcome, and knowledge to acquire. The ruling goddess of the month is Hestia, who helps us create a solid foundation for the journey ahead.

The Lunar Cycles

Despite their differences, all of the ancient Greek calendars measured time in units of years, months, and days, according to the cyclic nature of the sun and the moon. One year was marked by a complete seasonal cycle based on the Earth's revolution around the sun, while the year was divided into lunar months that followed the moon's revolution around the Earth (from new moon through full moon to new moon). Lunar months consisted of 29 or 30 days and were divided into three 10-day periods.

The lunar months consisted of auspicious days dedicated to specific gods, and inauspicious days during which no ceremonies would take place and certain activities would be avoided. Whereas in modern, Western paganism, we often celebrate the new moon and full moon, the ancient Greeks performed multiple rituals during the lunar cycle, which illustrates the importance of the moon's phases in ancient times.

The most important of these celebrations was the new moon ritual known as *Noumenia*, which was dedicated to Apollo and all household gods, including Hestia, Zeus, Hermes, and Hekate. Apart from the religious household ritual that people performed during the new moon, this was also a time during which they'd cleanse their statues and various ritual items, reorganize, and reenergize the altars.

You'll learn more about the significance of new moon and full moon and how to perform rituals during these phases in subsequent chapters.

CHAPTER 23

Performing Rituals

The ancient Greeks honored the gods and goddesses by performing a series of public and household rituals throughout the year. As mentioned in the previous chapter, different city-states celebrated different gods and festivals each month. The public rituals were usually grand events celebrated by the entire city-state and were performed in three stages—the procession, sacrifice, and prayer. In contrast, household rituals didn't have a set structure but were instead devised by and practiced around the hearth by the family unit.

For the purpose of this book, I'll share guidelines for performing household rituals in the way I've learned as part of my research, training, and personal preferences, but feel free to adjust and make these your own.

Ideally, a great way to connect with the gods and goddesses is to perform a monthly ritual celebrating the month's festival (usually on the last Sunday of the month), as well as new moon and full moon ceremonies at the start and the middle of the month. This way, you have three touchpoints in each month during which you can deepen your connection with the gods. Additionally, these are great opportunities to maintain your connection with the Earth's cycles through the year, but also to incorporate healing, manifestation, and other intentions into these rituals.

That being said, you don't have to perform all or any of these rituals if you don't feel called to. Given the demands of modern life, it may not be possible for you to carve out time three times each month for a ritual. Instead, pick and choose the festivals you feel are most important and focus on these. Similarly, if you can't do both a new moon and full moon ritual every month, pick the one that's most important for you and stick to that.

However many rituals you choose to do, in this chapter I'll share with you practical guidance for preparing for and performing your rituals. This will involve setting up a household altar. If you choose to do all three rituals each month, I suggest that you maintain the altar as it is after each ritual as a way of preserving the energy you've nurtured. You can dismantle the altar and create a new one the day you're about to do the next ritual. If you choose to not do any rituals at all, then I recommend that you set up a generic altar with Hestia as the main household goddess, as well as any other gods you want to connect with. You can mix and match the gods accordingly, as you feel guided to.

Creating Sacred Space

The most important element to performing any ritual is creating a sacred space that aids your connection with the gods. According to the *Encyclopaedia of Religion*, "A sacred place is first of all a defined place, a space distinguished from other spaces. The rituals that people either practice at a place or direct toward it mark its sacredness and differentiate it from other defined spaces."

A common debate among scholars of sacred space is the extent to which it is natural or manufactured. The three main viewpoints are:

- Sacred space is an ontological given in certain naturally sacred places.

- Sacred space is a social construct of certain rituals and practices.

- Sacred space is embodied and experienced on a personal level; that is, anyone can create it around their personal energy.

In my experience with studying sacred space from both a spiritual and an academic perspective, I've reached the conclusion that rather than being mutually exclusive, these three processes are all correct, and work in unison for the creation of sacred space.

Whereas there are certain places on our planet that are natural portals of divine energy, their sacredness and the degree to which their divine energy is utilized varies according to how we use them both as groups and individually. For example, although the Oracle of Delphi is a place of ontological sacredness, the rituals performed there by groups of people, as well as individuals having solitary spiritual encounters, add to its sacredness.

Consider also the town of Glastonbury, UK, and specifically the Glastonbury Tor. The Tor is built at a crosspoint of two major ley lines, the Michael and Mary lines, representing the Divine Masculine and Divine Feminine energies. Therefore, the Tor is a natural conduit of divine energy. However, the sacredness of the space is only fully experienced during some sort of spiritual activity—meditating, working your magic in a spell, doing yoga, or participating in a group ritual.

Conversely, a group of people participating in a ritual within a space, or even isolated individuals conjuring up the sacred through personal spiritual experiences there, opens up a portal of divine energy in that space. In time, that specific place transforms into an ontological conduit of spirit. An example is the Camino de Santiago in Spain. Although not an ontologically sacred space, the practice of pilgrimage over hundreds of years has turned it sacred, and many pilgrims each year report their spiritual transformations as a result of taking the journey.

In other words, sacred space exists as an ontological given, it is constructed through repetitive social practices, and it's also conjured by you, at any point, with your intention. When combined, these three practices can create powerful sacred spaces that open the door to divine communication. Keep them in mind while constructing sacred space through your altars in the next section.

Setting Up Altars to the Gods

An altar is a portal between the sacred and the profane. It is a bridge between the spiritual and earthly realms—a creation that aims to bring the gods into the physical realm so we can have an easier, deeper interaction with them. Therefore, setting up an altar opens up a portal to the spirit world and eventually transforms a secular space into one that is sacred.

Altars have been used by most indigenous traditions around the world, including the ancient Greeks. Since the beginning of time, humans have felt the need to communicate with the spirit world and have built physical altars with the aim of channeling and communicating with the nonphysical realm.

What to Include on the Altar

There are many schools of thought around setting up altars. In this section, I'll share what we know about ancient Greek altars coupled with tips from my personal experience.

Place

Although outdoor altars were common in classical times due to the layout of ancient houses, it may be more convenient to set up your household altar indoors. You can set up your altar on any surface in any room of the house. It could be on a side table in your bedroom, a shelf on your bookcase, a corner of your office desk, or simply a corner of the floor. However, I suggest that you set up your altar in a quiet space in a common area, especially if you plan on performing the rituals with the entire family.

Shape

Traditionally, Greek altars were rectangular. However, feel free to give your altar a shape that has meaning for you and for the god or goddess you're working with. It could be a circle, square, pyramid, star, or any other shape you feel inspired to use.

Altar Cloth

Setting up your altar on a piece of cloth is a symbolic way to set its extent and boundaries. It's also a simple way to transform a secular surface to something more sacred. Choose the colors and materials of your altar cloths mindfully so that they make sense for your chosen god or goddess.

Hearth

Our modern lifestyle doesn't always allow for a hearth to be permanently lit in the house, so the next best option is candles, an oil lamp, or even an electronic candle or lamp if you want to avoid fire completely. Always use natural substances, such as beeswax and soy wax candles or olive oil for the lamp.

Cleansing Water

Known as *khernips*, cleansing water is used specifically for cleansing and purifying our energy before we perform any kind of ritual. You can make it yourself by using either spring water or saltwater and setting the intention that it clears and purifies your energy. It's important to avoid using tap or stagnant water, and always drain and clean the bowl following the ritual. You can learn more about creating cleansing water in my book *Protect Your Light*.

Statues

During rituals, the statues are more than just representations of the gods; they embody the gods' essence and should be treated with the utmost respect. Although you can purchase statues for affordable prices from many online retailers, you can also use any sculpted or unworked natural materials as statues for the gods. For example, you can choose stones, crystals, and pieces of clay or wood. In fact, in the archaic period Greeks used *xoana* (singular *xoanon*) to honor the gods, which were often uncarved pieces of wood.

If you choose to purchase your statues, it's important that you choose statues depicting the god's or goddess's whole body rather than their busts or replicas of vandalized statues depicting the gods with missing limbs and other damage (most of which were performed by the early Christians).

Although statues are helpful aids to connecting with the gods, they aren't essential for your ceremonies, and you don't need to include them if you don't want to. Your intention to connect with the gods is the most important component of the ritual.

Ritual Dagger

Similar to the Wiccan *athame*, a ritual dagger is used symbolically to protect the altar from negative intentions, people, and energies. You can use any dagger for this purpose, but it's best to choose something that looks and feels sacred to you and that you use only as part of your ceremonies.

Storage

Near your altar, you may dedicate an additional surface or storage space for the statues (if you choose to include them) and other ritual items. It's important to have specific ritual items used solely for your ceremonies, and consecrate them using the practice in the next section.

Incense

The ancient Greeks used different incenses to honor each god, many of which you can find in the "Symbolism" section of each god's chapter. Traditionally, they used a tripod burner to burn the incense and other offerings, but you can use any burner you prefer. Personally, I've handmade a ceramic tripod burner, as well as most of my ceremonial tools, in my pottery class. If you have the time and energy to make your own ritual items, it's a great way to add your own personal essence to them and deepen your practice.

Offerings

Although the ancient Greeks often sacrificed animals to the gods, this is no longer a common practice. Instead, we now offer grains, fruits, and flowers as a way of acknowledging, showing gratitude, and reaching out to the gods. For this purpose, have a tray or a bowl that you can use to make your offerings during the ritual and potentially leave on the altar table. I often arrange a selection of grains in a tray in a visually appealing way and leave it on my altar until the next ritual.

Libations

A *libation* is the ritual pouring of a liquid—usually red wine, olive oil, honey, milk, or water—in honor of gods, heroes, other minor deities, and the dead. For this purpose, have a large bowl to pour in your libations, and another vessel to store the liquid. When offering a libation to the Olympian gods, you should always use red wine, while for *chthonic* (subterranean) deities, minor gods such as the Muses and the Nymphs, heroes, and the dead, you should instead use milk mixed with honey, or water. Libations to chthonic gods and the ancestors (known as a *choe*) are poured directly into the earth rather than your altar libation bowl.

Additional Items

In addition to or in lieu of the traditional ritual items used by both ancient and contemporary Greek pagans, feel free to make the altar your own by arranging and decorating it in a way that's aesthetically pleasing and feels right to you. Remember, you're setting up a sacred space to help you commune with the gods. The more personal you make it, the easier it'll be for you to connect.

A great way to bring life into your altar is to include natural items, which I like to call gifts from nature. Such items may include crystals, stones, soil, flowers, leaves, shells, sea glass, tree bark, fallen branches, or anything else you're guided to collect from the natural world. Always be mindful not to dismantle any animal's shelter or home. Walk softly upon the land and take only what you're intuitively guided to, with love and respect in your heart. If you feel guided to collect flowers or plants, it's important to intuitively ask them for permission before you cut them, and do so only if you get a yes.

Laying Out Your Altar

Setting up your altar is a ritual in and of itself. Once you have all the items and have spent some time planning how you want it to look, lay down your altar cloth, and with intention, prayer, and ceremony, place each item on the altar. Notice how you feel while setting up your altar, and include only items that inspire a sense of joy and upliftment. You'll know when your altar is complete by the emotion you *feel* when it's done! You'll feel a sense of completeness or open-heartedness and joy along with reverence, as the items you've placed create the perfect energetic combination to bring in your chosen god's energy.

Consecrating Your Altar

Consecrating your altar means to purify the energy of both the space the altar is set up in and the items you've included. Physical space and the items you've chosen all absorb vibratory frequencies from their surrounding environment as well as the people who have interacted with them (the ancient Greeks called this *miasma*, which means energetic pollution). Consecrating your altar resets the energy of everything so it can better align with the energy of the gods.

Follow these steps to consecrate your altar:

1. Start by practicing the Meditation Prep Process from Chapter 8 and bring yourself into a meditative state.

2. Choose your cleansing tool. There are many cleansing elements and tools you can use to cleanse your altar and ritual items. The most common cleansing aids used in ancient Greece were fire (in the form of sage and incense) and water (usually seawater or flowing water from springs and rivers), but you can also use sound (such as bells and gongs), essential oils, or your inner light channeled through your hands.

3. Bring your chosen tool/s close to your heart. With eyes closed, call upon the oversoul of the tool to activate its power and support you in this process. Intuitively, you may feel your tool vibrating or lighting up in some way, signifying it's ready to use.

4. Use the tool to cleanse your altar space in an intentional, ceremonial way. For example, if you're using lit sage, wave the smoke above, below, and around your altar with the intention that it's cleansing all negative energy.

5. After you've cleansed the altar, do the same for all the ritual items. Take each item one at a time and use your chosen tool to cleanse and purify it from all negative or residual energy.

6. When you feel the space and your ritual items have been consecrated, place the tool close to your heart and thank it for its assistance.

Activating Your Altar

After you've consecrated your altar, the next step is to dedicate and activate it so it serves as a sacred space to strengthening communication between you and the gods you're revering.

Follow these steps to activate your altar:

1. Start by practicing the Meditation Prep Process from Chapter 8 and bring yourself into a meditative state.

2. Place both of your hands on your chest and focus your attention in the center of your heart. Visualize a bright golden light extending from your heart

outward and into your palms. This is your own inner light and life-force energy.

3. Extend your hands outward to face the altar, visualizing the light washing over all the altar pieces and the surrounding space, instilling it with your loving energy and intention. Stay here for as long as it takes for your altar to feel elevated.

4. Dedicate the altar to the gods you're working with by saying and changing the call to the appropriate god: "I call upon [name of the gods] to enter this space and render it sacred, creating a clear portal of communication between the physical and spiritual realms. Thank you, and so it is."

5. When you're done, place your hands on your chest to end the process and ground your energy into the Earth.

Animating the Statues

As I mentioned earlier, statues aren't just representations of the gods, they act as gateways for the gods' presence during the rituals. They embody the gods' presence. Before they can take on this function, you need to *animate* them, meaning to invite the gods represented to bless and embody them.

Here's the process to animate the statues:

1. Having cleansed the statues, prepare a tray or bowl of a mix of grains, known as *panspermia* in Greek.

2. With intention, circle the tray over each statue in a clockwise direction while reciting the god's Orphic hymn (which you can find in the gods' respective chapters) and pour the grains on the statue.

3. While doing so, visualize the gods' light entering and activating the statues, blessing them with their presence.

4. Once you're done, your statues are animated and ready to be used in your ceremonies.

Dismantling the Altar

Before you perform a new ritual, it's important to dismantle your altar from the previous one, then consecrate and ground the energy of your altar space. The dismantling process should be carried out with the same sense of ceremony and reverence as setting up your altar, to show your gratitude for the work you've done with the gods.

Follow these steps to dismantle your altar:

1. Start by practicing the Meditation Prep Process from Chapter 8 and bring yourself into a meditative state.

2. Slowly and ceremonially, remove each item from the altar, holding it in front of your heart and silently thanking it for the role it played in your ritual.

3. Having dismantled your altar, use one or more of the consecration tools you used previously to cleanse the altar pieces and space, preparing them for the next ritual.

Now that you know how to set up and dismantle your altars, in the next chapters I'll share guidelines for performing your monthly festival rituals, as well as the new moon and full moon rituals.

CHAPTER 24

Monthly Festival Ritual

Since the ancient Greek religion wasn't standardized and didn't have central religious texts, its ceremonial proceedings varied greatly. Concurrently, a great deal of religious information was safeguarded within Mystery Schools, and most of the information that was made available at the time didn't survive the course of history.

Consequently, modern Greek pagans have used the little information we have about religious practices and created new ceremonial proceedings. Although these proceedings draw from the past, they're also supplemented with contemporary practices, contributing to the evolution of the religion. The ritual guidelines I share in this and the following chapters combine ancient practices, processes I've learned from the pagan communities I'm involved with, as well as my personal experience drawing from my spiritual journey.

Since there isn't a set way to perform these rituals, feel free to adjust them as you see fit and make them your own.

How to Perform the Monthly Festival Ritual

You can use the following steps to perform all monthly festival rituals and adapt them to the month's venerated gods. Before you get started with any ritual, make sure that you follow the steps in the previous chapter to lay out, consecrate, and activate your altar.

1. **Cleanse yourself.** It's important that you thoroughly cleanse yourself before each ritual by showering your physical body and clearing your energy. You can learn more about energy clearing in my book *Protect Your Light*. Entering the ritual with your energy as pure as possible not only is a way of respecting the gods, but also allows you to connect more deeply with the gods' essence and the festival's deeper meaning.

2. **Get into a meditative state.** Use the Meditation Prep Process in Chapter 8 to relax, center, and ground your body. Take a few extra minutes to clear your mind in meditation, and then ponder the meaning of the ritual you're about to perform as well as the essence of the gods you'll work with. These steps will ensure you're energetically protected but also fully present during the ritual.

3. **Cast a circle of protection.** Start by holding your ritual dagger near your chest, connecting with its energy and thanking it in advance for helping you cast a protective circle for the ritual. With your altar in the center, stand facing north with the altar behind you, and use your dagger to draw an energy circle clockwise around the periphery of your altar. As you move from north to east, south, and west around the circle, pause at each direction and say out loud, "Begone, begone all that is wicked!"

   Visualize the energy you draw stretching outward and forming a complete sphere around your altar. Mentally or out loud, set the intention that this energy sphere marks the boundaries of your sacred space and that only loving people, entities, and energies can enter it.

4. **Start the ritual.** To start the ritual, face your altar and, with hands extended to the sky, invite the gods you're working with to enter your sacred space. You can improvise an invocation or use the following: "I call upon [name of the gods] to enter this sacred space and guide this ritual." After the invocation, make a libation of red wine.

5. **Light the hearth.** Dedicated to Hestia, the hearth is an essential component of all Greek rituals. It serves as the heart of your altar, keeping the energy of the ritual activated, centered, and grounded throughout. While

you're lighting it, whether it is a candle, oil lamp, or another kind of fire, visualize the inner light within your heart lighting up as well, aligning you with Hestia and the energy of the altar. Having lit the hearth, extend your hands to the sky and recite the Orphic hymn to Hestia, ending it with "And so it is."

6. **Place the offerings.** Continue by placing your tray or bowl of offerings on the altar, depending on what these are. These usually consist of a mix of grains, fruits, and flowers, but you can also include crystals, plants, stones, and other tokens and symbols associated with each god. Refer to the gods' chapters for ideas.

7. **Light the incense.** Light the charcoal in the burner and add some incense to start the ritual. You can consult the gods' specific chapters to choose incense associated with each god, or use the incense you prefer. Besides the incense being an additional offering to the gods, due to its ethereal essence incense smoke transforms the profane into the sacred. It speaks directly to our primordial sense of smell, activating emotions and memories and helping us soften the boundaries between the physical and spiritual worlds. You can visualize the rising smoke's plumes as your prayers and intentions rising up to reach the gods.

8. **Recite the hymns and make libations.** Continue by reciting the two Orphic hymns of the month's god and goddess. Depending on the festival, you may want to include additional gods' hymns. For example, the Anthesteria festival is dedicated to Dionysus, despite Poseidon and Demeter being the gods of the month, and the Herakleia festival is dedicated to Hercules, while the gods of the month are Ares and Aphrodite. Therefore, do your research for each festival and bring in gods and goddesses associated with it.

It's customary to burn some of the god's specific incense (or your chosen incense) before you recite the hymn. While reciting the hymn, make sure you have both hands stretched to the sky, or have one hand on your chest and the other toward the sky. End each hymn with "And so it is," and continue by pouring a libation into your libation bowl (for Olympian gods) or the earth (for minor and chthonic gods, heroes, and ancestors).

9. **End the ritual.** End the ritual by appreciating the gods in advance for their blessings by improvising a farewell or using the following: "Farewell, [name of the gods]. Thank you for guiding this ritual, for your continued presence and blessings. And so it is." Finally, make a final libation of red wine.

10. **Open the circle of protection.** Using your ritual dagger and walking in a counterclockwise manner, open the energetic circle of protection and bring down the boundaries of your sacred space.

When the ritual is completed, you can leave the offerings on the altar for as long as you feel called to and then recycle them into the earth. You should never treat the offerings and libations as refuse or waste.

At the end of the ritual, you may use your journal to make notes of your impressions or any guidance and intuitive downloads you have received. It's also a good idea to take a few more minutes to center and ground yourself before you continue with your day.

CHAPTER 25

New Moon Ritual

As explained earlier, the new moon was known as *Noumenia* in ancient Greece. It's the first day of each lunar month marked by the appearance of the first silver of the moon. It was held in honor of Apollo Noumenios and the household gods, Hestia, Zeus, Hermes, and Hekate. In the words of Plutarch, the *Noumenia* is the "holiest of days," and no other religious festivals or governmental meetings would take place on this day.[1]

In antiquity, the new moon ritual served the purpose of starting afresh by setting intentions for the month ahead, very much like the way we approach new moon rituals in the West today. The new moon was also a great time to cleanse and update the home altar, incense the statues, and renew the offerings in the various altars of the house. Therefore, the new moon energy inspires reflection, introspection, and new beginnings. It's an opportunity to think about what you wish to create, achieve, or release, and sow the seeds to help you do so.

Consequently, in the new moon ritual that follows, I've included a manifestation practice that helps you leverage the auspicious energy of the new moon while connecting with the associated gods and goddesses.

How to Perform a New Moon Ritual

The steps to performing the new moon ritual are the same as the monthly festival ritual ones, with the addition of the following manifestation practice after the recitation of the hymns and before the closing of the ritual.

I've also included the Orphic hymn to Hecate that wasn't included in Part II.

New Moon Manifestation Practice

The aim of the new moon manifestation practice is to manifest, or make sufficient progress in manifesting, specific desires within the duration of the lunar month.

Here are the steps of the manifestation practice:

1. **Choose specific desires.** The biggest mistake people make when choosing new moon desires is choosing too many and too substantial desires. When these don't manifest by the end of the month, they lose hope and give up on their practice. For the purpose of this ritual, I suggest that you choose three specific desires that are unlikely but possible to manifest within 30 days. "Unlikely" means that you're pushing yourself out of your comfort zone to choose something big, but "possible" means that they're not too big to manifest within the month.

2. **Write down your desires.** Take a piece of paper and a pen and write down your desires in an affirmative way, as if they're already manifested or in the process of doing so. To do this, start each desire with "Thank you for . . ." Writing down your desires this way helps you believe in their manifestation and gets the gods and the Universe working toward that.

3. **Recite the hymn to Tyche.** *Tyche* (meaning "good fortune") is the Greek goddess of luck and good fortune; therefore, she's a great goddess to invoke along with the rest of the *Noumenia* gods to help manifest your desires. Remember to burn incense before you recite her hymn and make a libation of red wine afterward. You can find her Orphic hymn in the following section.

4. **Run your desires through smoke.** Next, fold the piece of paper with your desires, burn some incense of your choice, and run your desires through the

smoke. While you do so, visualize the energy of your desires rising up with the smoke to reach the gods.

5. **Surrender your desires to the gods.** Finally, surrender the outcome of the manifestation practice to the gods by placing your piece of paper near the statues on your altar. Trust that the gods will support you in manifesting your desires.

Orphic Hymn to Hecate

Lovely Hekate of the roads
and of the crossroads I invoke.
In heaven, on earth,
then in the sea, saffron-cloaked,
tomb spirit reveling
in the souls of the dead,
daughter of Perses, haunting deserted places,
delighting in deer,
nocturnal, dog-loving,
monstrous queen,
devouring wild beasts,
ungirt and repulsive.
Herder of bulls,
queen and mistress of the whole world,
leader, nymph,
mountain-roaming nurturer of youths,
maiden, I beseech you to come
to these holy rites,
ever with joyous heart,
ever favoring the oxherd.

Orphic Hymn to Tyche

I summon you here through prayer,
Tyche, noble ruler,

gentle goddess of the roads,
for wealth and possessions,
I summon you as Artemis the guide,
renowned and sprung from the loins
of Eubouleus,
your wish is irresistible.
Funereal and delusive,
you are the theme of men's songs.
In you lies the great variety
of men's livelihood:
to some you grant a wealth
of blessings and possessions,
to others you bring evil poverty
if you harbor anger against them.
O goddess, I beseech you,
come in kindness to my life,
grant me happiness,
grant me abundant wealth.

CHAPTER 26

Full Moon Ritual

Full moon festivals in ancient Greece consisted of all-night festivities reserved almost exclusively for women, and were in honor of the moon goddesses Selene, Artemis, and Hecate. Although we don't have further guidelines about the full moon ritual proceedings, I've used what we know to design a full moon ritual that honors the moon goddesses while also supporting the manifestation of the desires you've come up with during the new moon ritual.

Whereas the new moon is all about new beginnings, the full moon is about culmination. During this time, the gravitational pull of the moon is at its highest, causing the tides to rise and pulling soil moisture to the surface to amplify plant growth. Since we're made out of water, we're also affected by the gravitational pull of the full moon. During this time, emotions run high, challenges come up, and life intensifies in every way. As a result, this can be an intense and overwhelming time.

Simultaneously, the bright energy of the full moon also makes this a time of abundance, manifestation, and illumination. However intense and challenging of a time it may be, the full moon energy also amplifies our creative power, allowing us to bring our desires to life. Consequently, performing a full moon ritual is a way for us both to release upsetting and overwhelming thoughts, habits, and emotions and to celebrate our manifestations thus far.

How to Perform a Full Moon Ritual

The steps to performing the full moon ritual are the same as the monthly festival ritual ones, with the addition of the following letting go practice after the recitation of the hymns and before the closing of the ritual.

I've also included the Orphic hymn to Selene after the practice.

Full Moon Letting Go Practice

The aim of the full moon letting go practice is to surrender your manifestation expectations for the desires you've come up with during the new moon, and allow the magical and potent energy of the full moon and her goddesses to take control of the process.

Here are the steps to the letting go practice:

1. **Read your desires.** Unfold the piece of paper with the desires you've written during the new moon ritual and read them to refresh your memory. While you do so, notice how you feel about them. Do you feel grateful for the ones that have manifested? Do you feel frustrated with or worried about the ones that haven't manifested yet? Acknowledge and be present with these emotions, noticing whether they're helping the manifestation process or not.

2. **Acknowledge the progress.** If all your desires have manifested, congratulate yourself and continue with the rest of the ritual! If some or all of your desires haven't manifested yet, take a few moments to acknowledge the progress you've made so far. Have you received any evidence of the desires being in the process of manifesting? What actions have you taken toward their manifestation? Manifestation is a collaborative process between you and the Universe; you have to do some work, too! Have you manifested something similar? Or have your desires changed or expanded in some way?

3. **Let go of expectations.** Whether these desires manifest or not within the lunar cycle isn't entirely up to you. Apart from the Law of Attraction (also known as the Law of Vibration), there are other laws in the Universe that

affect the manifestation process. Realizing this helps you let go of the outcome and trust the process. To deeply let go of your expectations, declare the following out loud: "Whether [name of the desire] manifests or not, I deeply and completely love and accept myself. I trust that there's a higher plan in place, and that this or a better desire will manifest at the perfect time, when I'm ready."

4. **Burn the desires.** To fully let go of your expectations for results and let the power of the full moon and the associated goddesses take over, burn the piece of paper with your desires in a ceramic or other fireproof container. At the end of the full moon ritual, make sure to bury the ashes into the ground or scatter them in the wind.

Orphic Hymn to Selene

Hear me, O divine queen,
O light-bringing and splendid Selene,
O bull-horned Moon,
crossing the air as you race with night.
Nocturnal, torch-bearing,
maiden of beautiful stars, O Moon,
waxing and waning,
feminine and masculine,
luminous, lover of horses,
mother of time, bearer of fruit,
amber-colored, moody,
shining in the night,
all-seeing and vigilant,
surrounded by beautiful stars,
you delight in the quiet
and in the richness of the night,
you grant fulfillment and favor
as, like a jewel, you shine in the night.
Long-cloaked marshal of the stars,

wise maiden whose motion is circular,
come, O blessed and gentle lady,
lady of the stars, through your own light
shine and save, O maiden,
your new initiates.

EPILOGUE

The last three months of writing this book have been hectic! While my deadline was approaching fast, I was memorizing lines for drama school exams, rehearsing weekly for my debut in a Greek production of *Mamma Mia*, launching *Intuition Mastery School*, running my business, and also trying (not so successfully) to have a social life. As a result, during this time I almost completely abandoned my spiritual practice, which made me feel like an impostor.

Here I was writing about setting up altars, following the Greek Wheel of the Year, and performing moon rituals, while my altar was gathering dust, I'd skipped the last three monthly festivals, and I had no idea what moon phase we were at, let alone performed a ritual about it! As much as I craved connection with the gods, I simply didn't have the time to do any of that at that moment. And I felt awful about it!

On one of my writing days late at night, I was digging through my mountain of books searching for something, when I stumbled upon the handwritten notes I'd made during my initial priesthood training in 2017. It read, "The gods are within everything; they're not separate from us. They don't exist; they simply *are*. They don't have form; *we* created that so that we can better communicate with an *aspect* of them. Therefore, by definition, personifying the gods diminishes their essence."

As I read that, it hit me—I don't really need to perform rituals, make offerings, and set up extravagant altars to connect with the gods. I simply need to perceive them within me, within others, and within the world. Yes, I enjoy carving out the time to set up altars, perform rituals, and meditate at ancient temples, but these practices simply complement my connection with the gods; they don't establish it.

Our connection with the gods doesn't need to be established, because we aren't separate from them. The Universe is an ocean of the gods' essence and we're swimming in it. All we need to do to feel the gods' presence and receive their blessings is to consciously seek it in the here and now.

Wherever you are right now and whatever you're doing, stop, close your eyes if possible, and take a deep breath in. While you breathe in, affirm "Wake up!" and set the intention of waking up the divine within you. Take a few more deep breaths while repeating this affirmation, and focus on experiencing the divine essence of the gods and goddesses within you. Open your eyes and observe other people and the world around you, noticing the divine essence of the gods and goddesses within them, too. Perceive beyond the physicality of your surroundings and realize that the gods' essence flows through every single piece of consciousness within and around you.

I do this exercise whenever I find myself feeling disconnected from myself and the gods. It instantly tunes me in and gives me perspective on the true essence of my spiritual practice. Although I'm now back on my usual monthly ritual routine, I know that no matter what life throws at me or how busy my schedule gets, I'm part of an ocean of pure, loving, and divine wisdom, and that's all that truly matters.

Receiving Signs

A nother way of communicating and deepening your relationship with the Greek gods and goddesses is by asking for and receiving signs from them. The gods and the spirit world in general are constantly reaching out to us in whatever way they can, sending us signs and imparting guidance to help us follow our purpose, manifest our desires, and live our best life. Although the signs and the guidance are constantly coming in, the degree to which we can receive them depends on our level of intuitive development.

I've been consciously developing my intuitive abilities ever since I was 15 years old. Although I wasn't born "gifted," I've worked hard and consistently to develop my abilities and do this work for a living. Today, I'm a professional psychic healer and also train others to advance their abilities and become professional psychics as part of my five-week online program, *Intuition Mastery School*.

I believe that talent is overrated and we can all develop any skill we want if we're passionate about it and put in the work. In this and the following appendix, I'll share with you my top tools and practices for developing your intuitive abilities so you can receive clear signs and guidance from the gods and goddesses.

Sign Interpretation in Ancient Greece

Divination held great importance in ancient Greece. Before launching a war or making an important decision, state officials would usually get a prophecy from one of the famous oracles at the time.

At the Oracle of Delphi, the *Pythias* (singular *Pythia*) were priestesses to Apollo who would go into a trance state and deliver messages from the god. At the Oracle of Dodona, the *Selloi* were priests that conveyed Zeus's will to mortals through signs they received in their dreams. The divination modalities practiced at the oracle also included the interpretation of animal sounds (particularly birds), the murmurs of water flowing under Zeus's sacred oak tree, and the ringing of bronze cauldrons.

Furthermore, the Oracle of Zeus at Olympia was known for *pyromancy* (divination by fire) and the Oracle of Demeter at Patrai for *catoptromancy* (divination by mirror) and *hydromancy* (divination by water).

Aside from the famous divination oracles, such as the Oracles of Delphi, Claros, and Dodona, and incubator oracles, such as the Asklepieion at Epidaurus, the ancient world was also rife with *mantises* (singular *mantis*), independent prophets who used various divination modalities to receive signs and messages from the gods. Oftentimes, generals and statesmen had their own independent mantises to consult them during wars and other state matters.

The mantises often used a wide variety of divination systems to receive and interpret the gods' signs. A few of the most popular practices used were throwing sheep knucklebones (acting as dice), paying attention to chance utterances such as body twitching and sneezing, and reading animal entrails.

Types of Signs

Whereas the ancient Greeks interpreted specific kinds of signs and manifestations, anything and everything can be a sign from spirit. What makes something a sign has to do with the nature of and way through which we receive the signs. As a rule of thumb, signs from spirit tend to be unusual but possible, and unexpected.

They're unusual but possible in the sense that they stand out from the mundane world in some way, but they're also within the realm of possibility. For example, you don't often see holographic cars out in the streets, but they do exist (Paris Hilton has one!), so seeing a holographic car is unusual but possible.

Signs are unexpected in the sense that you don't go out looking for them. Instead, they show up when you least expect them. In the example of the car, going out and actively finding a holographic car doesn't count as a sign. But if you unexpectedly see one without consciously searching for it, that could indeed be a sign.

Although anything can be a sign if you want it to be, we've collectively associated certain items and occurrences as signs from spirit. Here are the most common signs people receive:

- Feathers
- Animals

- Butterflies
- Repeated numbers (11:11, 444, 21:21, etc.)
- Coins
- Clouds
- Songs
- License plates
- Flowers
- Rainbows
- Billboard signs and ads
- Flickering lights
- Words in books and articles
- Orbs in photos
- Meaningful dreams

How to Receive Signs

One of the most common obstacles people face when receiving signs from the spirit world is doubting the signs they receive. As soon as they receive something they identify as a sign from spirit, their ego immediately comes in to doubt it. As a result, they second-guess the sign and their intuition, and they're left feeling frustrated.

Use the following process to eliminate doubt by asking for and receiving clear signs from the gods:

1. **Frame your question.** When we ask for a sign from spirit, it's usually because we're unsure about something, need to make a decision, or want a confirmation about our chosen path. Before you ask for a sign, frame a specific question that can be answered in a binary way. For example, you can ask, "Should I go down this path?" or "Is this the right thing for me at this time?" or "Am I making the right choice?" Alternatively, you can frame your question in a statement like, "Give me a sign that I'm making the right choice."

The rule of thumb here is to frame your question in a way that can be easily answered with an affirmative sign. When it comes to your binary questions, the sign you receive will count as a yes. The gods can certainly provide guidance for more general, open-ended questions as well, but this will usually come through more advanced intuitive practices, which I discuss in the next appendix. Signs are best suited to simple, binary questions.

2. **Choose a specific sign.** As I explained earlier, signs can come in many different forms. Your ego will grab any opportunity to doubt the signs you receive as chance occurrences, unless you're specific about the sign you want to receive. The more specific you are about the sign you want to receive, the less likely your ego will be able to doubt it.

   Thus, when choosing a sign, make sure you follow the guidance in the previous section, and that it's something unusual but possible for you to receive. It doesn't necessarily have to be within the list of the most common signs I included. Feel free to choose something that's unique or meaningful for you.

3. **Set a timeframe.** Waiting for a sign can be really frustrating, especially if you're on a deadline with making a decision. Therefore, it's always a good idea to set a specific timeframe during which you want to receive a sign. Ideally, have it be between 3 and 24 hours to give the gods enough time to organize it.

4. **Get out and surrender.** If you've chosen a holographic car as your sign, you probably won't see it unless you get out of the house. Sure, you may see a picture of it online, but your ego will jump in right away and tell you it didn't count because it was only a picture! Make it easy for the gods to communicate with you. Give yourself enough opportunities to receive your chosen sign during the course of your set timeframe by getting out of the house and engaging with the world. That being said, be mindful of not actively searching for the sign. Instead, surrender your expectation for it and let it show up when you least expect it.

What If You Don't Receive the Sign?

If you've followed these guidelines but haven't received your sign, it could mean a couple of things. First, not receiving a sign could be a negative answer to your question. Remember, we're asking for affirmative signs, so not receiving a sign automatically counts as a no. Second, you may have indeed received a sign but missed or doubted it. This could be because you've chosen too rare of a sign or because your ego sabotaged the process. If you think this may be the case, troubleshoot what went wrong and repeat the process with a new sign for a maximum of two additional times.

Receiving Intuitive Guidance

If you're ready to go beyond just receiving signs from the gods to receiving more in-depth intuitive communication from them, you have to invest time and energy in developing your intuitive abilities. As I've shared previously, I teach advanced intuitive development in my online course *Intuition Mastery School*. In this chapter, I'll share a beginner's guide to intuitive development to get you started on your path.

What Is Intuition?

Encyclopedia Britannica defines intuition as "a natural ability or power that makes it possible to know something without any proof or evidence." Therefore, intuition doesn't belong to a few gifted people. It's our sixth sense, and we can all learn to use it consciously to receive knowledge and guidance from the gods, our higher self, and the spirit world. Although we're all born with it, some people are more talented at using it or have been given more opportunities to strengthen it.

Because intuition isn't easy to observe or study scientifically, the scientific community and the modern world in general have largely disregarded it. As a result, most of us haven't been taught to access our intuition and don't know how to leverage it for receiving intuitive guidance and communicating with the spirit world.

How Intuition Works

Your intuition's sense organ is your third eye chakra. In the same way that you use your eyes to see, your ears to hear, your hands to touch, your mouth to taste, and your nose to smell, you use your third eye to receive intuitive messages. Like all seven chakras, your third eye chakra is an energy portal in the center of your head between your eyebrows, and it's linked to perception, awareness, and intuitive communication.

What makes intuition tricky to study in relation to the other senses is that although the other five sense organs are primarily responsible for receiving sensory perceptions (i.e., the eyes are responsible for seeing and the nose for smelling), the third eye receives intuitive guidance via the other five senses and chakras, too. For example, although you can receive intuitive guidance solely via your third eye, you can also receive intuitive guidance in the form of visions, sounds, sensations, tastes, and smells.

Therefore, your third eye acts as a control center and receives intuitive guidance via your five senses and chakras. The relationship between the third eye and the other senses has resulted to what's known as the six *clairs*, intuition types, or intuition languages.

Your Intuition Type

Your intuition type is the primary way through which you receive intuitive guidance. Although the third eye uses all five senses to receive intuitive messages, most people have one or two senses that are more activated than the others. Of course, we can develop all intuition types if we wish to.

Here are the six intuition types, or clairs:

- Clairvoyance (clear seeing)
- Clairaudience (clear hearing)
- Clairsentience (clear feeling)
- Clairgustance (clear tasting)
- Clairalience (clear smelling)
- Claircognizance (clear knowing)

The first five clairs correspond to the five senses, while claircognizance is connected to the crown chakra and has to do with the intuitive sense of knowing something. Finding your dominant intuition types is an essential step to developing your intuition, as it will simplify the process of accessing your intuition and receiving guidance.

How to Find Your Intuition Type

While the best way to find your intuition type/s is through practice and experience, the following questions will help you gain more clarity:

- Close your eyes and recall your most recent birthday party. What were you doing and where were you? What happened, and who was there? Play through the entire event in your mind.

- What is your favorite childhood memory? Allow yourself to go back and fully remember it.

- What was your proudest achievement? Return to the moment when you accomplished it. How was the experience? Who did you tell? What happened next?

Spend some time replaying these three events in your mind or journaling about them. All of these were times in your life when your sensory system was especially stimulated. Through what senses did you experience these events the most? Did you mostly see, feel, hear, taste, smell, or know how things unfolded? Which senses were the most active?

Once you find out what your intuition types are, it's just a matter of paying more attention to them when receiving signs or intuitive messages. You can also consciously strengthen your intuition types or develop new ones if you wish to. You can learn practices to do so in my book *Be the Guru* and my online course *Intuition Mastery School*.

Ways of Receiving Intuitive Messages

Now that you know your dominant intuition types, you're ready to start using them to receive intuitive guidance from the gods and goddesses. There are many ways to go about this, but I've included what I consider to be the three most effective practices.

Using Divination Systems

Oracle tools and divination systems are powerful ways of communicating with the gods and goddesses. Such systems include tarot and oracle card decks, runes, tea leaf readings, and dowsing using a pendulum. Although there are ancient Greek divination systems you can use, too, such as *cleromancy* (divination by throwing lots or dice), *hydromancy* (divination by water), and *pyromancy* (divination by fire), they aren't the easiest to practice for someone just starting out. I recommend starting out instead with one of the more established divination systems just mentioned.

The easiest of these systems in my experience are tarot and oracle card decks. There are many different card decks to choose from, many of which are based on the Greek gods, Greek mythology, and spirituality. These will allow you to receive specific messages from the gods in a physical way that your ego won't be able to doubt.

Tarot and oracle cards work on the principle that when you ask a question, the gods will select the most pertinent cards from the deck to answer it. Even so, some level of interpretation is still necessary because various people will interpret words, symbols, and even visuals differently. Knowing how uniquely our subconscious minds operate, I have never trusted symbol and tarot dictionaries. A black cat might be a negative omen for one person and a positive one for another. Thus, I've always been a proponent of reading the cards in an intuitive way—that is, being aware of your senses as you draw a card and interpreting its symbolism using your main intuition types.

I would advise working with oracle cards first before switching to tarot if you have never used cards as a divination system previously. This is because tarot readings need specialized knowledge and practice, but oracle card readings are far simpler to perform.

Practicing Automatic Writing

Automatic writing involves asking a question and allowing the gods to give you the answer intuitively in words or drawings. During automatic writing, you let the gods flow through you to merge with your consciousness and communicate their message. These always arrive to you as intuitive impressions through your dominant intuition types.

Unlike spiritual possession during which a spirit takes over your body, with automatic writing you have full awareness and control over yourself, and you're responsible for translating the guidance in written form. The mental and energetic state of asking a question is different from the state of receiving the answer, and automatic writing helps you easily switch between the two. When practicing automatic writing, you first ask the question and then consciously get into a state that allows you to receive the answer.

Use the following steps to practice automatic writing:

1. **Frame your question.** Unlike the binary questions for receiving signs, with automatic writing you can ask more general and open-ended questions in any way you want to. Ideally, though, you should stick to one question at a time so you receive more focused guidance. Get a piece of paper, start a note on your phone, or open a document on your computer and write down your question.

2. **Get into a meditative state.** Start with Chapter 8's Meditation Prep Process and then spend some time getting into a deep state of meditation. This will allow you to raise your vibration to the frequency of the gods so that you can best facilitate communication with them.

3. **Shield your energy.** This step is important to keep your energy protected from unwanted spirits and energies. You can ask Athena to activate her shield within your aura, Apollo to shield you with his golden light, use any of the shielding practices in my book *Protect Your Light*, or leverage any other energy shield you prefer.

4. **Ask the gods to take over.** Depending on the god/s you want to communicate with, ask them to merge with your energy and impart their guidance. To do so, visualize their light or energy entering your body through your crown chakra and saturating your body and energy.

5. **Automatically write.** Keeping your mind and body relaxed, open your eyes, get your pen or device, and start answering the question you've written down. The key for making this process work is to write continuously for at least three minutes without allowing yourself to stop and consider what you're writing. Anything you think, see, hear, feel, taste, or smell, and anything that happens around you from the moment you start writing onward, is intuitive guidance.

While you write, pay special attention to the guidance that comes through your dominant clairs. If you know you're clairvoyant, be mindful of the visions that come in your mind or the visual signs that spirit may be showing you in your surrounding environment. Of course, be aware of all your clairs, as you may receive guidance in a variety of ways, but in my experience when we pay extra attention to our dominant clairs, especially in the beginning, we make ourselves feel more comfortable and at ease, allowing for a more effortless flow of intuitive guidance.

Is It Intuition, or Am I Making Things Up?

The most common block people face when receiving intuitive guidance is doubt. As I mentioned previously, your ego will do whatever it takes to sabotage the process and keep you from communicating with the gods. Once you know the ego's ways, you can learn to distinguish between real intuitive messages and the ego's interference.

Here are three ways to distinguish between ego and intuitive guidance:

- **Intuition comes first, while ego comes next.** Intuitive guidance is usually the first thought you get. It comes quickly and spontaneously, while ego guidance tends to come in shortly after to sabotage your intuition.

- **Intuition feels expansive, while ego feels contractive.** When you receive intuitive guidance, your body agrees with it. You'll feel an expansive, positive feeling within your body. When the guidance comes from your ego, you'll feel a negative feeling and your body contracting.

- **Intuition feels certain, while ego feels doubtful.** You never doubt or question intuitive guidance. You instantly trust it and take action toward it. Conversely, ego guidance feels doubtful. This is when you make pro and con lists and ask other people's opinions about it.

Whenever you catch yourself doubting your intuitive guidance, go through these three indicators to get clarity. If you end up getting confused, take a break from the whole thing and ask for a clearer sign. It's always easier to get new guidance than to analyze old guidance. The gods will happily send an avalanche of signs your way until you get it.

For more guidance on developing your intuition, check out *Intuition Mastery School* at *www.IntuitionMasterySchool.com*.

ACKNOWLEDGMENTS

To the 12 Olympians, thank you for trusting me with your wisdom and guiding the writing of this book. It's an honor to follow your guidance and walk your path.

To Vlassis Rassias, thank you for generously sharing your wisdom through your books and teachings. Your courage and dedication to the resurgence and legalization of Hellenic Polytheism paved the way for all of us.

Thank you to all my friends and fellow priests at the Supreme Council of Ethnic Hellenes (YSEE) for supporting and guiding me through my priesthood journey.

To my friends and peers Emma Mumford, Hannah Wallace, Amy Leigh-Mercree, and Tammy Mastorberte, thank you for your unending and unconditional support while I was writing this book.

To my best friend, Sargis, thank you for joining in my craziness and accompanying me on a temple-hopping trip around Greece. I couldn't have taken this journey with anyone else.

Thank you to Sahara Rose, Amanda Yates Garcia, David Wells, Shereen Oberg, Amy Leigh-Mercree, Emma Mumford, Danielle Paige, Victoria Maxwell, Sophie Bashford, Ananta Ripa Ajmera, Cael O'Donnell, Sergio Magaña, Tammy Mastorberte, Julie Parker, Anjie Cho, and Pamela Chen for your generous endorsements and support.

Thank you to my agent, Lisa Hagan; my publisher, Michael Pye; Eryn Eaton, Maureen Forys, Christine LeBlond, Kathryn Sky-Peck, Brittany Craig, Rachel Monaghan, and the entire team at Hampton Roads for placing your trust in me and this book.

Thank you to Mike Willcox for the stunning artwork on the cover!

To you, the reader, thank you for joining me on this journey to learn about and live with the Greek gods and goddesses.

NOTES

Chapter 3

1 Although Dionysus was sometimes considered an Olympian god instead of Hestia, he isn't one. Dionysus was a relatively newer god and hasn't reached Olympian status. Therefore, he's not included in the book, but we do celebrate him in the Anthesteria festival (see Chapter 22).

Chapter 9

1 Plato, "Definitions," in *Plato: Complete Works*, ed. John M. Cooper and D. S. Hutchinson (Indianapolis: Hackett, 1997).

2 Aristotle, *Nicomachean Ethics*, trans. Hugh Tredennick and J. A. K. Thomson (New York: Penguin, 2004), 4.3.

3 Translations of hymns throughout the book are from Apostolos N. Athanassakis and Benjamin M. Wolkow, trans., *The Orphic Hymns* (Baltimore: Johns Hopkins University Press, 2013), 5, 11, 16–19, 25, 28, 30, 32, 35, 44, 53, 57, 64. © 2013 Apostolos N. Athanassakis and Benjamin M. Wolkow. Reprinted with permission of Johns Hopkins University Press.

Chapter 10

1 Plato, "Definitions," in *Plato: Complete Works*, ed. John M. Cooper and D. S. Hutchinson (Indianapolis: Hackett, 1997).

2 Antoine Fabre D'Olivet, Antoine Fabre Pythagoras, and Nayán Louise Redfield, eds., *The Golden Verses of Pythagoras* (New York: G. P. Putnam Sons, 1917).

3 Xenophon, *Memorabilia*, trans. Amy L. Bonnette (Ithaca, NY: Cornell University Press, 1994).

4 Plato, "Definitions."

Chapter 11

1 Hesiod, *Theogony and Works and Days*, paperback ed., trans. and ed. M. L. West (Oxford, UK: Oxford University Press, 2008), line 885 of *Theogony*.

2 Plato, *Phaedo*, paperback ed., trans. David Gallop (Oxford, UK: Oxford University Press, 2009).

3 Andrei Zavaliy, "Andreia," *ODIP: The Online Dictionary of Intercultural Philosophy* (2020), ed. Thorsten Botz-Bornstein, *odiphilosophy.com*.

4 Michelle E. Brady, "The Fearlessness of Courage," *Southern Journal of Philosophy* 43, no. 2 (2005): 189–211.

5 Plato, "Definitions," in *Plato: Complete Works*, ed. John M. Cooper and D. S. Hutchinson (Indianapolis: Hackett, 1997).

6 Plato, "Definitions."

Chapter 12

1 Hesiod, *Theogony and Works and Days*, paperback ed., edited and translated by M. L. West (Oxford, UK: Oxford University Press, 2008).

2 Monica S. Cyrino, *Aphrodite* (Abingdon, UK: Routledge, 2010).

3 Herodotus, *The History*, trans. George Rawlinson (New York: Tudor Publishing Company, 1936); Nancy Serwint, "Aphrodite and Her Near Eastern Sisters: Spheres of Influence," in *Engendering Aphrodite: Women and Society in Ancient Cyprus*, Vol. 7, ed. Nancy Serwint and Diane Bolger (Boston: American Schools of Oriental Research, 2002), 325–50, *jstor.org*.

4 Diogenes Laërtius, *The Lives and Opinions of Eminent Philosophers*, trans. Charles Duke Yonge (London: G. Bell and Sons, Ltd, 1915), *gutenberg.org*.

5 Iamblichus, *Life of Pythagoras, or Pythagoric Life*, trans. Thomas Taylor (London: J. M. Watkins, 1818).

Chapter 13

1 *Hubris* (ὕβρις) is an ancient Greek word that originally conveyed a sense of outrageous conduct or acts that violate the bounds set for humans by the gods. Over time, it has come to represent extreme pride or arrogance, especially toward the gods, or defiance of the natural order. The concept is deeply embedded in Greek literature, especially in tragedies where characters' hubris often leads to their downfall.

2 John Burnet, *Early Greek Philosophy*, 3rd ed. (London: Adam & Charles Black, 1920).

3 Burnet, *Early Greek Philosophy*.

4 Burnet, *Early Greek Philosophy*.

5 Peter Critchley, "Pythagoras and the Harmony in All Things," 2011, *academia.edu*, accessed October 24, 2023.

Chapter 15

1 Aeschylus in *Tragicorum Graecorum Fragmenta*, 2nd ed., trans. August Nauck (Leipzig, Germany: Teubner, 1889), Fragment 70.

2 Plato, "Definitions," in *Plato: Complete Works*, ed. John M. Cooper and D. S. Hutchinson (Indianapolis: Hackett, 1997).

3 Morris Stockhammer, ed., *Plato Dictionary* (Totowa, NJ: Littlefield, Adams, 1965), *archive.org*.

4 Plato, *The Republic*, trans. Desomond Lee (London: Penguin, 2007).

5 Xianzhong Huang, "Justice as a Virtue: An Analysis of Aristotle's Virtue of Justice," *Frontiers of Philosophy in China* 2, no. 2 (2007): 265–79, *www.jstor.org*.

Chapter 16

1 Hades and Pluto are the same god. The name *Hades* was used in earlier antiquity and later came to be synonymous with the underworld, while *Pluto* was used in later years and had a more positive connotation.

Chapter 17

1 Plato, "Definitions," in *Plato: Complete Works*, ed. John M. Cooper and D. S. Hutchinson (Indianapolis: Hackett, 1997).

2 Isocrates, *Isocrates with an English Translation by George Norlin in Three Volumes* (Cambridge, MA: Harvard University Press; London: William Heinemann Ltd., 1980).

3 Arrian, *Flavii Arriani Anabasis Alexandri*, 5.26.4 (Leipzig: A. G. Roos. in aedibus B. G. Teubneri, 1907).

4 Hans von Arnim, ed., *Stoicum Veterum Fragmenta* 3.264 (Stuttgart, Germany: B. G. Tuebner, 1964).

5 Plato, "Definitions."

Chapter 18

1 Aristotle, *Politics*, trans. Carnes Lord (Chicago: University of Chicago Press, 2013), Book 7.

2 Matthew Gonzales, "The Oracle and Cult of Ares in Asia Minor," *Greek, Roman, and Byzantine Studies* 45, no. 3 (2005), grbs.library.duke.edu.

Chapter 19

1 Plato, "Definitions," in *Plato: Complete Works*, ed. John M. Cooper and D. S. Hutchinson (Indianapolis: Hackett, 1997).

2 Joannes Stobaeus, "Sentences of Demophilus," in *Florilegium*, vol. 1 (Leipzig, Germany: Teubner, 1855), 117 (Peri Sophrosyne 42).

3 Helen North, *Sophrosyne: Self-Knowledge and Self-Restraint in Greek Literature* (Ithaca, NY: Cornell University Press, 1966).

4 Cicero, Tusculan Disputations, trans. Charles Duke Yonge (New York: Harper, 1877), 3.8.16, gutenberg.org.

5 Euripides, *Hippolytus*, trans. Robert Bagg (Oxford, UK: Oxford University Press, 1973).

6 Drew A. Hyland, *Plato and the Question of Beauty* (Bloomington: Indiana University Press, 2008), 105.

7 Kirsten Weir, "Nurtured by Nature," *Monitor on Psychology* 51, no. 3 (2020), apa.org.

8 Joseph G. Allen, John D. Macomber, and Suzanne Labarre, "We Spend 90% of Our Time Inside—Why Don't We Care That Indoor Air Is So Polluted?," *Fast Company*, May 20, 2020, www.fastcompany.com.

9 Richard Kraut, "7. Akrasia," in *Stanford Encyclopedia of Philosophy*, ed. Edward N. Zalta (Summer 2017 edition), plato.stanford.edu.

Chapter 20

1 Sharon Lebell, *The Art of Living: The Classical Manual on Virtue, Happiness, and Effectiveness* (New York: HarperOne, 2007).

2 Seneca, *Letters from a Stoic: A Guide to the Good Life—the Complete 124 Revised Letters*, ed. Alexandre Pires Vieira, trans. Richard Mott Gummere (Indianapolis: Montecristo Publishing, 2020).

Chapter 25

1 Plutarch, *Moralia,* trans. Arthur Richard Shilleto (London: George Bell and Sons, 1898), 828a 8, *www.gutenberg.org*.

SELECTED BIBLIOGRAPHY

Allan, Arlene. *Hermes*. Abingdon, UK: Routledge, 2018.

Aristotle. *The Nicomachean Ethics*. Translated by Hugh Tredennick and J. A. K. Thomson. New York: Penguin, 2004.

Aristotle. *Politics*. Translated by Carnes Lord. Chicago: University of Chicago Press, 2013.

Athanassakis, Apostolos N., and Benjamin M. Wolkow, trans. *The Orphic Hymns*. Baltimore: Johns Hopkins University Press, 2013.

Budin, Stephanie Lynn. *Artemis*. Abingdon, UK: Routledge, 2015.

Burkert, Walter. *Greek Religion: Archaic and Classical*. Hoboken, NJ: John Wiley and Sons, 2013.

Burnet, John. *Early Greek Philosophy*. 3rd edition. London: Adam & Charles Black, 1920.

Cooper, John M., and D. S. Hutchinson, eds. *Plato: Complete Works*. Indianapolis: Hackett Publishing, 1997.

Cyrino, Monica S. *Aphrodite*. Abingdon, UK: Routledge, 2012.

Deacy, Susan. *Athena*. Abingdon, UK: Routledge, 2008.

D'Olivet, Antoine Fabre, Antoine Fabre Pythagoras, and Nayán Louise Redfield, eds. *The Golden Verses of Pythagoras*. New York: G. P. Putnam Sons, 1917.

Dowden, Ken. *Zeus*. Abingdon, UK: Taylor and Francis, 2006.

Graf, Fritz. *Apollo*. Abingdon, UK: Taylor and Francis, 2009.

Hellenic Council YSEE of America. *Hellenic Ethnic Religion: Theology and Practice*. Athens: Hellenic Council YSEE of America, 2016.

Hesiod. *Theogony and Works and Days*. Translated and edited by M. L. West. Oxford, UK: Oxford University Press, 2008.

Johnston, Sarah Iles. *Ancient Greek Divination*. Hoboken, NJ: John Wiley and Sons, 2009.

Μαρίνης, Παναγιώτης. *Η Ελληνική Θρησκεία*. Αθήνα: Νέα Θέσις, 2002.

Nauck, August, trans. *Tragicorum Graecorum Fragmenta (TrGF)*. Leipzig, Germany: Teubner, 1889.

Panopoulos, Christos, Panagiotis Panagiotopoulos, and Erymanthos Armyras. *Hellenic Polytheism: Household Worship*. Athens: LABRYS Polytheistic Community, 2014.

Plato. *Phaedo*. Translated by David Gallop. Oxford, UK: Oxford University Press, 2009.

Ρασσιάς, Βλάσης Γ. *Αρετή: Το Αξιακό Σύστημα Των Ελλήνων*. Αθήνα: Ανοιχτή Πόλη, 2012.

Ρασσιάς, Βλάσης Γ. *Αρετή: Το Αξιακό Σύστημα Των Ελλήνων*. Αθήνα: Ανοιχτή Πόλη, 2016.

Ρασσιάς, Βλάσης Γ. *Περί Των Πατρώων Θεών*. 3rd ed. Αθήνα: Ανοιχτή Πόλη, 2018.

Sallust, *The Gods and the World; the Pythagoric Sentences of Demophilus; Five Hymns by Proclus*. Translated by Thomas Taylor. Los Angeles: Philosophical Research Society, 1976.

Taylor, Thomas, trans. *The Hymns of Orpheus* (1792). Philadelphia: University of Pennsylvania Press, 1999.

Three Initiates. *The Kybalion*. Bishop Auckland, UK · Aziloth Books, 2010.

Τουτουντζή, Ουρανία Ν. *Ἄρτεμις*. Αθήνα: Ανοιχτή Πόλη, 2022.

Von Arnim, Hans, ed. *Stoicorum Veterum Fragmenta, Volume 3: Chrysippi Fragmenta Moralia Fragmenta Successorum Chrysippi*. Stuttgart, Germany: B. G. Tuebner, 1964.

Xenophon. *Memorabilia*. Translated by Amy L. Bonnette. Ithaca, NY: Cornell University Press, 1994.

ABOUT THE AUTHOR

GEORGE LIZOS is a spiritual teacher, psychic healer, Greek pagan priest, creator of *Intuition Mastery School*®, as well as a #1 bestselling author (*Be the Guru, Lightworkers Gotta Work, Protect Your Light*) and host of *The Lit Up Lightworker* and *Can't Host* podcasts. He helps lightworkers overcome the fears and limiting beliefs that prevent them from finding and following their life's purpose of finding happiness, helping others to heal, and ascending the vibration of the world.

He has been named one of the top 50 health and wellness influencers, and his work has been featured in *Goop, MindBodyGreen, POPSUGAR, Soul & Spirit, Spirit & Destiny, Kindred Spirit,* and *Watkin's Mind Body Spirit* magazines. He holds bachelor's and master's degrees in metaphysical sciences, a BSc in human geography with a focus on sacred geographies, an MSc in psychology, an MSc in business management, and a diploma in acting.

George took part in the first official priesthood training in Hellenic Polytheism organized by the Supreme Council of Ethnic Hellenes (YSEE) in Athens following the religion's legal recognition by the Greek government in 2017. Since then, he's been a practicing priest of the religion at the world's first modern temple of Zeus in Cyprus. George has taught about the Greek gods and spirituality in his books, workshops, and online courses, and his research on Aphrodite has been published by *Soul & Spirit* magazine and *The Numinous.*

www.GeorgeLizos.com
www.YourSpiritualToolkit.com
Instagram: @georgelizos

Get Weekly Tools

Download my FREE *Discover Your Life's Purpose* guide to find and define your life's purpose in a specific, two-paragraph definition. You'll also receive my weekly newsletter with more tools and guidance. Get it at *www.GeorgeLizos.com/lifepurpose*.

Work with Me

If you've enjoyed this book and want to go deeper, check out my online courses, meditations, and private sessions at *www.GeorgeLizos.com/work-with-me*.

Get Support

Meet like-minded lightworkers, learn new spiritual practices, and attend exclusive workshops within my private Facebook group, *Your Spiritual Toolkit*.

Feel Inspired

My *Lit Up Lightworker* podcast features interviews with leading spiritual teachers on various spiritual topics, while my *Can't Host* podcast provides guidance and education on sex and relationships for gay, queer, and bisexual men. Check them out on Apple Podcasts, Spotify, and all main podcast platforms.

Stay in Touch

Tell me all about your experience with connecting with the gods and goddesses on Instagram (@georgelizos).

TO OUR READERS